The Realization of Creation

The Loving Light Books Series

Also by Liane Rich

Loving Light

Book 13

The Realization of Creation

Liane Rich

The information contained in this book is not intended as a substitute for professional medical advice. Neither the publisher nor the author is engaged in rendering professional advice to the reader. The remedies and suggestions in this book should not be taken, or construed, as standard medical diagnosis, prescription or treatment. For any medical issue or illness consult a qualified physician.

Loving Light Books
Original Copyright © 1994
Copyright © 2010 Liane

ISBN 13: 978-1-878480-13-2
ISBN 10: 1-878480-13-8

Loving Light Books:
www.lovinglightbooks.com

Also Available at:
Amazon: www.amazon.com
Barnes & Noble: www.barnesandnoble.com

"If you judge it you kill it! You cut off the flow of energy when you judge and it stifles all of creation. Stop judging you and you will continue to rejuvenate and reproduce your own self, to the extent that you become eternal beings as you are meant to be."

The information in this series is not necessarily meant to be taken literally. It is meant to *shift* your consciousness....

The Realization of Creation

Introduction

You are now among the few who know that creation is only a perception and that all creation must be realized in order to perceive on any given level. As you begin to perform your duties as creator of any given creation, you must realize how you affect creation. You are, at one time, the creator and the created. How can the creator have no effect on its creation and how can creation have no effect on its creator? Also... who owns who? Does creation own its creator or does the creator own creation?

We have now brought you back to that age old question of who came first. Was it God or was it a creation that exploded into realization and universal awareness? How many of you are aware that you are God and how many of you are aware that creation is the creator? How many of you are conscious at this moment and how many of you believe you are conscious when, in actuality, you are quite unconscious and not even here yet?

So, who is God and who is creation? Are you not God and do you not belong to creation? Are you here or are you not yet arrived? How much of you is in you and how much of you is even real? How long can you pretend to be what you are not and how long can you survive without acknowledging who you really are?

You are the creators of a world much grander than any you have ever experienced in your present state of unconscious behavior. Once you have fully regained your true identity which, of course, is God in all his glory, you will be truly astounded to realize how far out you went in order to discover what was always there and what was always known. You will find that as you begin to fluctuate back and forth between the conscious realization of your own creation and the unconscious wisdom that is yet arriving, you will become a bit confused and maybe even nauseous. You see, in fluctuating back and forth you convince yourself that things are one way and then re-convince yourself that things are really the other way. This could make for some pretty contradictory beliefs which challenge the flow. Now you are here and a minute later you are there. Now you believe and a minute later you do not.

You are a contradiction in terms in that you cannot be pinned down to one way or the other. This is due to the fact that you are everything and everything is you. You will change and fluctuate and move and transform and you will still be you, all of you. You are the totality of "all that is." You are both sides of the fence and everything that makes up the middle. You have no end, you have no beginning and you never ever stop being at any given moment. You are *all that is,* you are not one or the other. There is no such thing as God or man, there is simply love. Love is God and love is man. One is not more valuable than the other. The creator is no greater than his creation and creation is no less than its creator.

So, who is God, me or you? You decide and that will be your reality for now. It has always been so. Man chooses what he wants to believe and then he forces his belief onto others so he can feel safe with it and not alone in case he is wrong.

≈⫸⫷≈

If you will begin to allow for your own use of creation you will see how you are even becoming creation. You are part of this vast, complex system that is known as God and you do not know what you are. Many of you do not know what you are in terms of body and you really don't have a clue when it comes to spirit. You know you have a skeletal structure and that you are tied together by tissue and muscle and arteries, but beyond that you know, or even care to know, little about how you function.

The average person is so besot by the onslaught of civilized life that he/she cannot fully understand how to be, let alone how to unravel the complexities. Most of you are so wrapped up in trying to feel good about yourselves on a day to day basis that you do not even realize the vast potential that is growing within you. You are pawns in a game and you feel used and pushed around and out of control. The more out of control you get the more you fight to hang on to your old identity. The more you fight to hang on the more stress you feel, as you are being stretched to let go.

This is the process that is known as birth. You want to stay where you are, but you must move on out of the womb. This warm vacuum, which you have sprung from seed in, is collapsing around you and it is only because this part of your growth is accomplished. You are being born and leaving the protection of the womb behind. Yes, it is nice and cozy and you don't have to worry about being supported by life as you have all that you need right here.

In order to grow you must leave this safe place and go out into creation and learn to walk and to talk and to run and to play. You will not be hurt if you do not choose to. You will find that the majority of you will not be well or happy in creation. The majority will be sick and sad. It is the fear. The fear that allowed you to believe that you were not God is the fear that has inflicted you with illness since the beginning of time. If you knew unequivocally that you are God you would never be sick, or sad, or afraid.

It is only your fear of being God that keeps you from coming home to God. It is only your fear of being God that keeps you away from God. It is only your fear of the unknown that keeps you in what you think you know. Let go of what you think you know and move into what you don't want to know. All your answers are in you and you do not want to know you because you are afraid to face God. You are afraid you will have nothing left if you face God. The truth is, you have always been God, you simply do not wish to admit it. It is so much easier for you to say, "Oh, I'm so bad, I have sinned" or "Oh, I'm so awful and so stupid." You have the evil role down, now I'd like to see you play the divine role. Stop acting evil and begin to act divine.

You are not God in hell, you are God in creation. You are not evil on earth; you are divine spirit entering into flesh. Give up the role of sinner. Stop judging until you know what's really going on here in creation. Do you know what creation is all about and what is about to occur? If you do not, how can you possibly play the role of judge? Stop judging and allow your life to become what it is meant to become. Do you know what your life is meant to become? If your answer is no, then I suggest you allow your life to unfold without judging it as bad. You are in you for a reason and you are drugged. Allow yourself to be guided until you have enough consciousness to drive your own body. You are in no condition to drive, so God is revoking your keys until you get it together.

You must recall how you got here in order to return. Do you remember? Do you have conscious memory or are you just stumbling around looking for a way out of your confusion? Either way you have not failed and you have not erred, you have simply lost your memory, so I am reminding you ever so gently and I am nudging you back toward me. You are returning and ascension is well on its way and you feel it, but you judge it as chaos and pain. You always fear what you do not understand and what you do not understand you then label "bad," "evil," "wrong," "horrifying." Give it a rest. If anything is horrifying in all of this it is the condition you are in. You are totally drunk and unaware that you are God. We must sober you up and remind you of your position and your loyalty and your love and your power.

Some cold water in the face may help or maybe to slap you enough to get you to walk a straight line. You keep stumbling into the same old pits and you keep staggering from here to there and back again. You are also screaming obscenities and if I could just calm you all down enough I could explain that there are not giant pink elephants or any other giant things that want to harm you. You are in a drugged state so you don't see what is really in creation; you see your own state of mind projected back to you. You are drunk, you are drugged; I must get you sober. Talking to you in this state is like speaking to a terrified child who only wants to feel safe.

So for now, I will tell you that you are safe. You are coming out of the womb and you will be safe. You will grow to be big and strong and very lovable. You are God being born and you will like being God.

⁂

You are now at a turning point, and you will find that as you become more and more conscious you will begin to allow for more and more flexibility. You are in a state of moving and forming into God awareness and God consciousness. You have always been this awareness, but now you will show yourself what you have always been.

As you begin to unfold more and more of this unknown you, you will find yourself losing control, as this new you is no longer concerned with control. This new you does not care about being the best, as it is "all that is." This new you does not care about achievement, as it is "all that is." This new you does not care about being right, as it is "all that is." How can you worry about such details when you know that you are "all that is?" How can you care who does best when you know that you are "all that is?" How can anyone do less than another when everyone is part of "all that is?"

No one is better than and no one is less than. You may have achieved financial wealth or you may have achieved only little things like winning a bowling trophy. None of it matters. It is not achievement that matters. This, of course, is in direct conflict with all the teachings of the material world. It is taught that you must achieve success and you must achieve honor and you must achieve an education and you must achieve status. You must only "be." To "be" is already your achievement. To be in human form is quite an achievement in itself. You have achieved going backward and shutting down. You have achieved being dumb and blind to the fact that you are God.

To be God and convince yourself that you are not took a great deal of effort on your part. You must now reverse this process and become again what you have always been. You are not so afraid to be what you have always been as you are afraid to know what you have done in this process. This process took some time to lay itself in place and there are a great many restrictions involved. Most of these have to do with energy and how it is dense and used to reinforce your barriers and defense mechanisms to hold you in place – which is in *denial*.

You are now coming out of denial and one of the first things I wish you to know is that you need not *do* anything for you *are* everything. So, this is your lesson for today. You need not do or achieve anything, you already *are* everything!

❧

*A*s you begin to discover various parts of you that are just now emerging, you will begin to develop a new sense of who you are based on who you are becoming. You may begin to feel most uncomfortable with yourself and no longer understand your own behavior. It is all part of this process of ascension. We are bringing all parts of you to the surface and this will enable you to heal the illness, pain and disease of many generations.

As you become more and more secure with what you are doing, you will become less and less afraid to face you. You will become less afraid of your own emotions and your own power to deceive. You will also become less afraid of truth as you will be giving up deception and moving out of denial. As you reach this phase you will want to know that you are not alone. You may feel very much alone and like no one else is as frightened and confused from all of this as you are. This is not true. All are afraid and all are confused. Those who are coming up out of denial at this time may have a greater degree of fear that they are looking through, but none is untouched by ascension.

One of you may feel pain and confusion and be surrounded by friends who seem to be enjoying life to the fullest, with no concerns and no fears. All is not as it seems. Sometimes you draw these individuals just to show yourself how far you have come. You will look at such a friend and think "Wow, he/she has it all together. Why can't I?" This, of course, is you reflecting back to your self-judgment. You have it all together and it's all coming up and out to show you how well you are doing. You are bringing *up* all the energy that has blocked you from perfection and from the truth. Do not judge yourself for falling apart at the seams. You are becoming pliable and flexible and your seams were holding you in and restricting you.

So, for those of you who have fallen apart – "We salute you." You are moving very quickly and this is a good time to remind you that you are here to grow and change for God. This is not exactly how a human pictures growth, but this is the time of spirit, and spirit operates on a whole new and different level. You will find that spirit is often compelled to rise above the most mundane job and find joy in the simplicity of creation. God's ways are as simple as man's ways are complex.

So; now we have you falling apart and it is good to let you rest often. This is an important time for rest. I know you all teach about high energy, active roles and how to attain high levels of energy for yourselves, but for now I would like you to listen to your body and find time to rest when it is tired. This ascension process is very high energy work taking place within, and it requires a great deal of letting go and rebuilding of cellular structure. This tends to tire the body and I do hope you will listen when your body needs rest.

The next thing I wish to speak to you about is your diet. I require lots and lots of water during this process of ascension. It is lubricating all parts of this body that I'm working within. Drink as much as possible and drink it without gulping please. Just a nice steady flow of water on a daily basis will keep all body parts well lubricated, which will allow energy to pass freely through your body. But then you all know this already as you have all been doing enemas to move the energy through your bodies. Water is a great conductor of energy. If you do not think so, drop your hair dryer in the tub with you and see how fast you move. Water cleans and water moves easily, two very good things about water. Water is also very good for you. After all, you were kept in water for nine months before you entered earth. Water is an important part of your life.

Now that we have discussed water we will discuss your habits. Number one habit, is believing in death. Yes, this is a trained habit, a repeated teaching that created a result. Give up this habit as things are about to change. Number two habit, is believing in long-term suffering. Give up the belief that you must suffer or work hard for all of your life. Let yourself begin to create new habits to live by. You are so afraid to let go of the old because it is all you have known and so you hold on to it like an old habit that you cannot break. Now is the time to break old habits and to learn to create new habits. You are revolutionists and you are just now beginning the transformation process. It will begin to look as though you are in total chaos at some point. I know it looks that way now on your television news, but you are all experiencing this *shift* in consciousness and it is being reflected back to you through your view of your reality.

As you begin to move forward into change you will feel radical change, as radical change is what is necessary at this time. It is good to flow with all that occurs. Sometimes you are physically moved and other times you are mentally moved, but move you will. You see, we are all moving. This is moving day and we are moving from the third dimension into the fourth dimension. You will like your new home once you have let go of your need for your old surroundings and favorite things (habits) around you. You will learn new ways and find a much more loving and peaceful way to live within you!

☙❧

As you begin to become aware of your many attitudes and beliefs you will begin to discover an entirely new way to override the will of your habits. Most habits are based on a belief that was once hopeful or did a service in a certain area for you. If you discover that you have a belief that says, "I must be poor as I cannot have wealth and be happy" you will find that, at some point, you decided to believe this in order to survive or in agreement with your primary caregivers. If you have a belief that says, "I must be rich and have lots of money or I will never be happy," this too was put in place out of a fear or a need, and it will last until you decide to change your programming.

In either case, you are choosing one or the other and you must learn to let go of both types of belief. Both of these beliefs will cause imbalance within the body and will cause struggle within your life. The interesting thing is that some of you have both beliefs battling it out inside of you. One may have come from a parent or relative and the other may have been decided on by you, as a means of developing character different than that of the parent who carried the opposing view. If your parent believed strongly that wealth brings sorrow and unhappiness, then you may have developed the opposing view just because you did not want to end up like your parent.

This is called gaining experience through understanding the basics of energy. If you wish to outgrow or grow beyond your parental limitations, many of you may have developed a conflicting point of view. The interesting thing is that until you decide to change that particular view you also carry it as your own. You were connected to it through your parents, and you chose to break free of it when you chose to see things differently than your parents or primary caregivers. You may have decided to challenge a view at a very early age and therefore you have carried both views.

Not everyone is imbalanced in this way, but most are and most have this struggle within to overcome or override the programming of early childhood. The best way to overcome your beliefs is to allow everything to become a possibility. Allow everything to be good or at least okay. As you learn to allow being poor to be okay you will inadvertently be allowing wealth to be okay. They are the same energy. It is two sides of the same view, and the line meets in the middle and it all becomes one energy line with opposing forces. When you learn to accept poverty as a good thing you learn to accept wealth as a good thing. You cannot push wealth away and view it as bad or you will create that reality, and you cannot push poverty away and view it as bad or you will create that reality.

Some of you believe that you must only accept what feels good to you, and your feel-good feelings are all cross wired at this moment. This is why you have drugged yourselves and drunk yourselves into graves so often. You are smoking and fighting for your right to do so. You are drinking and hiding it if you must. You are doing every sort of drug imaginable and this includes your over-the-counter headache pills. You are a drugged-out creation, and I wish to get you to feel good without the pills and cigarettes and alcohol that you all feel you need. It is not what you need, it is an addiction to pain that keeps you causing greater pain. It is that struggle within that keeps you wound up and unable to cope.

Once we have you a little more balanced you will find it easy to give up your drug of choice and come back to reality. You are so drugged out that you will find it comforting to know that you will not have too great of a hangover when you begin to desist this type of activity. You are all drugged on some level and this is why your awareness is impaired. You will find that as you come out of your drugged state, you will return a great deal of awareness to your own consciousness.

As I began to channel through Liane, I found it necessary to stop her drinking and drug habits. She too drank quite often and took many prescription drugs. She was a mess psychologically and it took a very restricted diet to get her in condition to write these books. But, as you see, she got it together and continues to write for me, and continues to open new doors within her own self and to elevate her own awareness.

It is good to know who you are and to admit it freely. If you have a problem with your own identity you can always change what you do not like and keep what you do like. You are basically creating you as you go and you can have any identity you wish. Just think it and then proceed to become it. It may take a little time, but then time is all you have. You have lots and lots of time, so what do you want to do with it? Do you want to be who you are or do you wish to change? Do you like feeling how you feel or do you wish to feel good without drugs and without stimulants?

You can have it all, you know. You can have everything in balance with no good and no bad. No evil and no hate and bad feelings. Everything will simply become okay. Taking drugs is okay and dying is okay. They are simply two choices out of many. You get to choose how you want to be. You may have any choice from all the billions and billions of possibilities. You are creating you as you go, and you may choose to rise above the polarities of good vs. evil into the oneness of good.

Allow everything to be okay and you will find that you will be allowing you to be okay. I do not tell you to stop drugging yourself or else you will go to hell. You already are in hell and I say to you, "Here is the way out. Here is awareness of what you are doing. If you wish a way out become un-addicted." You will find that as you learn more and more about how you judge yourself you will also learn more and more about how you judge God. Do not put your mask on God and force words into God's mouth. God does not threaten, God teaches from awareness. It is as simple as saying, "If you drink too much you will have a very big headache." This is not a judgment call, it is a probability and it is a very likely one.

Now I am saying, "If you clean up your act you will feel better." This is not judging your act, this is again a probability, and it is a very likely one. So, begin to know you and begin to clean up your act. It's time now. If you wish to reach the fourth dimension in the first shift you will want to begin now.

*I*t is not a very good idea to allow yourself to be laid down to die. You might as well allow yourself to be put to death. Most of dying is an illness that you have not been able to heal. If you allow yourselves to heal, you will no longer suffer death. Death is a disease and it afflicts everyone. It is the most common disease you have. It is literally shared by all who live on Earth. Because everyone does it does not mean it is required. How can you be so foolish as to believe that a body must decay and die? If the body continually reproduces cells in every area, how can it decay and die as a natural part of its evolution? This is not natural.

As you begin to learn more and more about your own bodies, you will discover that you are an entire reproductive cell. You have the ability to reproduce and regenerate at will. You do not realize the extent of your ability to stay living. You need not age and you need not deteriorate. This is something that was created to get you out of here. You got tired of living in a cocoon and you wanted to move on. You know that there is much more than this three-dimensionally-restrictive reality and you saw no other way out. I am now telling you that there are many ways to transform yourself without destroying good matter.

One of the most highly evolved methods is ascension. It will bring you to a new level of perception which allows you to rise above the belief in death and deterioration. As you begin to rise above this old outdated belief, you will begin to see how you have always been and will always be, and how you are the Almighty God that you so aptly fear. Once you realize that it is all you, you will realize that if you are God and you created it all, why then don't you create what you want? Why not give yourself everlasting life and erase the illusion of mortality as a non-existent reality. Make immortality the new hip thing. Create as God would and often does create. God has no restrictions. God can make whatever God wishes. Are you game for this? Do you want to begin to believe in immortality of all, not just the soul but "all that is?"

You need not continue to kill off everything that you outgrow or become bored with. Civilizations need not die and certain strains of animals need not end. Transformation is on the rise. Do not kill it off; transform it into the next creation. No one need end ever. Everyone and everything just changes to the next thing or creation. Go to a movie and watch how you use a child actor to play the role of someone who twenty minutes later becomes an adult. So now you are watching this adult person, but you have no idea where the child went. You simply *know* that the child is still there inside the adult. Transformation is much the same. All parts are still there with a conscious awareness that they are. No one has left. The child is gone, but you do not mourn his loss as you know that he went inside the adult or he grew into an adult. Everything has the ability to grow into everything else. Upon your leaving this plane, where you are physically visible, you go into whatever you wish. You cross over from here to there and you last forever.

You are part of *all that is* and no part dies. You only pretend that you die in order to create a flow of creation. You don't want too many of you here at one time so you continually create this illusion that says, "It'll be okay, because when they die there will be more room." They are not dying to make more room. As a matter of fact, they don't want to die in most cases. So I say, "Stop the game." Begin a new game and call it "life everlasting." Stop creating death and begin to create everlasting life that moves and grows and transforms into whatever form it wishes. Begin to create creation to your liking and let go of the belief that you must do what you do not like.

Begin to know that you are the creator of your own creation and begin to know that you may create it however you want it. You all tell your children about this wonderful place called heaven, where there is no bad and everyone lives forever on nothing but love. This is the closest story you have to what truth really is. Don't kill off the story of heaven. Keep it alive and bring it down to earth. Keep heaven and leave hell. You have spent enough time believing in evil and awful and horrifying. You are so attached to these that you cannot let go and move to peace and love and calm.

Look at your favorite movies. Most are action films with lots of fighting and killing and destruction. Look at your junk papers or tabloids as you call them; lots of bad news and exploitation. You love gossip and you love to see the big guy fall and the little guy win. It thrills you. You are addicted to this type of rising up and getting revenge. The funny thing is that you create your "big guys" and then when they get too big you begin to find ways to tear them down, dig up their past indiscretions and find out all the dirt you can to disprove their wonderfulness.

This is how you live your lives. You give your own self credit and then you discredit your own good. You build you up and then you tear you down. You create and then you destroy all the good support you have given yourself. You build you up and then you tear you down. This is about to change and you will no longer find it necessary to destroy what you create. You will come to a point in all this where you decide to leave your creation alone and allow it to become whatever it is meant to become. This will be the moment of change. This will be transformation. This will be you letting go of your need to destroy whatever you create. This will be the day that the need for death will become a distant memory. "No more death, no more destruction. Heaven will be brought down to earth."

❧

*I*t is not long before you begin to realize how you are growing in awareness and learning to be all one. You will find that as you integrate your own perceptions into a vast consciousness, you become more and more capable of coping with life and of being alive. You are the hope for God. You are the birth of and the coming together of all parts of God. You are the one who is "becoming" and it will be quite an expansion process.

You will begin to develop slowly and you will graduate to new levels of awareness each time you let go of an old way of seeing life. You will learn that as you graduate to each level of consciousness you literally pull you up a notch, and you may position yourself for the next step and then move up again yet another notch. This is a slow but sure process and it works. It is like climbing a straight up-and-down cliff. You find a tiny foothold and you take it. You hold yourself in place as you reach for this tiny foothold, and once you have your foot securely planted you reach for the next hand grip or handhold. You do not want to stop climbing or your body will become rigid from the tension of holding yourself in place while you search for that next thing to hold on to, or the next place to securely step.

As you develop greater and greater balance and agility, you begin to climb more and more surely. You know you are learning this strange technique for climbing the face of a cliff, and you know you can succeed if you just stay calm and look for new places to step or hold on to. This is how you are climbing and rising today. You let go of one thing, be it money, or a person, or a bigger fear like death, and as you let go you begin to feel suspended and uncertain and you want to scream. Then you find a new foothold, maybe it is a new friend or a new sense of security that fills in for the money. Then you grab hold and think, "Okay, this is not so bad. I can survive without that."

Next, you begin to lose hold of something else you *thought* you desperately needed to be safe. And as you let go of it altogether you begin to flail about in mid air on the side of this cliff. This, of course, was a big letting-go-of so you are thinking how stupid you were to ever have done so. This is the big fear and you judge yourself harshly for letting your footing go and hanging only by your fingertips, as you thrash about in sheer panic.

Then, calm begins to return and you discover that, if you stay very quiet and focus on just your body, you can raise yourself up to the next available foothold and not lose total control and crash to your demise at the bottom of this cliff. So now you begin to focus only on survival and you let go of any other thoughts. Nothing else matters but you and what you do. This is the first time in your life that you have felt this need to take good care of you. You always thought you took good care of you, but you were never really focused on you, and you never thought much about your feelings and your fears until now.

So; here we have you hanging on the side of the cliff and you are desperately searching for your next foothold. You find a tiny groove in a rock and you slide your foot in. It begins to take hold and some of your trembling begins to subside, as you catch your breath and decide to reach for another hand grip that will help you feel more secure in your position. You now begin to move a little more quickly and are more trusting about letting go of old positions, because you know that the quicker you can calm your fears and move on, the quicker you will get to the top.

So; why did you begin to climb this cliff in the first place? You are being moved to go into your fears and face your fears in order that you may have a fear-free life. You wish to know fear in order to free you of the belief that fear is dangerous. You wish to learn to look at who you are, and, if you are fear, you will allow your fear to transform to awareness by showing it its way. You are teaching fear to grow into love by allowing it to express itself and showing it that fear is not the only way. You will find that, as you allow fear to move through you, it will begin to find its own way and it will leave you alone. Do not feel abandoned when fear goes. It is leaving now and many of you are feeling lost and alone. You see, fear has been your dear friend for a very long time. Now this friend is being replaced and you will have a certain amount of sadness regarding this. You will also be hurt and confused as your fears leave you one by one.

This is the beginning of understanding and awareness. You will come to develop a whole new way of viewing reality and it will be with the realization that everything is change and movement and growth. This is a great time of new dreams and very high hopes. This is a great time of knowing that all is as it should be. This is a great time of adjustment to a better way that you actually feared, and this is a great way to arrive in you.

You will find that as you begin to move into a state of conscious behavior, you will know more about you than ever before. You will begin to realize what you do and how or why you do it. The simplest things will begin to make sense and you will begin to unravel the mystery of you. As you move forward in your life, you will begin to notice how you are leaving out parts of you that in the past you have never wanted to leave out. Now, however, there doesn't seem to be a great need to express certain parts.

As this need to express certain parts begins to fade, you will find yourself replacing this with other, sometimes greater, needs to express other parts of you. As you learn to express these parts, you will be allowing them to be and you will open the doorway for even greater expression of unknown parts of yourself. This is all part of this evolution process and I don't want you to think that you are "losing it" or going "crazy." Well, actually, you are losing it and you are crazy! This, of course, is your perception of crazy and what you are losing is fear of expression.

As you begin to move into your next phase of evolution, you will find yourself being a little more cautious and a lot more expressive in a subtler fashion. As you become more and more subtle, you will gradually lose the need to express. It simply will not be a necessity. You will have outgrown it. You will not care whether or not you have a say in anything as it will not matter. You will be living from your own creative energy and it simply will not matter what is said, or what opinion is voiced, or who has a say in what.

God will be ruling and creating, and creation will know that it is safe and has nothing to fear from God and his ways. Once you reach this level of realization, you will have a great deal of peace and serenity. You will know that God is running the show and this will alleviate the need for protection, and transformation will be at hand. You will no longer find it necessary to vote and you will no longer find it necessary to debate. All such silliness will end.

As you begin to alleviate such unnecessary practices, you will have a better balance. Those who are over-achievers will begin to slow down and see how there is nothing to prove to anyone, and those who are under-achievers will begin to move into a position of knowledge that will allow them to move forward without restraint. Everything will come back into balance and everyone will come back into balance.

Now; before you reach this state of balance, you must clear those obstructions that have kept you unbalanced. In clearing these obstructions you will begin to go way out of balance. The closer to the surface your obstructions get, the more out of balance you will become. Then, after you have released the obstruction, you will feel much lighter and swing back into balance. This process will go on with each obstruction you carry. It must come up out of you and, as it does so, all of the relating tendencies will show themselves. No matter what the fear is it will be attached to, or related to, many other fears.

This is like a chain or string of things that are coming up out of you and, in some cases, the string or unbroken chain can be quite long. So, if you begin to feel like you haven't been "your self" for a very long time, it could be your very long chain coming to the surface to bring you balance and harmony.

You will find that as you achieve greater balance you will be achieving greater awareness. This is all part of the process; it is all part of becoming God. It is all part of the plan.

༄

As you begin to discover your true association with life, you will begin to see how you are linked in with every living being. You are part of everyone and everything else. Everyone and everything are connected. You are the one and only and you are "all that is." You are the vast majority and you are the single minority. You are the one who walks your path and you are the one who watches you walk your path.

Now is a time of uncovering this truth and making it known that you are "all that is." You are truly in a position to be of assistance to your own self, as you are the one who is creator as well as creation. When you begin to assist yourself, you will find that most of what you need assistance from is illusion. You are not only being put in a position of creator and creation, you are also in the position of the savior. You are saving you from the dread and uncertainty of a life of constant fear and continual confusion.

As you begin to save yourself from the bonds of fear and confusion, you will grow with wisdom and intelligence and you will begin to light up or illuminate. With illumination comes awareness, and with awareness all things are possible. As you become aware that all things are possible, you will be aware of God. You will be rising above limitation and you will be becoming "all that is." With possibility comes availability of resources. When you allow for availability of resources you allow for everything to coexist and you allow for God to be right inside you where he has always been.

With the coming of God comes the coming of power. As you begin to use your abilities, you will find it necessary to restrain yourself in certain areas in order to develop fully and properly. You will wish to know that I do not recommend running about screaming to your neighbors how you have God awareness and the power it brings. This may cause some unforeseen problems and you may end up right back in confusion. So, as you begin to arise from confusion into your awareness, take it easy and do not disrupt your life or the lives of others overly much. Allow yourself to know that you have shifted and begin to feel the subtle changes with great care. Remember, you are here to become God, but so is everyone else so let's not make too big of a fuss over it.

You will find that as you move into greater and greater depths within yourself, you will be focusing on greater and greater confusion. Then as you move into greater and greater levels of awareness, you will be floating to higher levels of freedom. Everything is attached to everything else. You are all one and God is in everyone and everything. It is eminently important to remain calm. This will assist you both in awareness and in confusion. Calm and serenity play a big role in this transformation and both will assist you in rising above chaos and confusion.

Now you are on a path that is directly connected to your inner dimensional self. As you walk this path you will begin to realize how you create certain situations and how you wish to create better, more loving situations in your future. You are learning now how to be you so that you might appreciate you. The old you was not greatly appreciated by you, so now you are putting in a second personality who you might find more acceptable and lovable. Give you a new face and you are happy for a while. So I give you a new face by showing you how multidimensional you are, and how you really have no reason to look down on yourself as yourself is truly glorious. In the beginning of this series you thought of yourself as a rock. Now you know that what you really have is pure gold and the ability to create whatever you want for yourself. You have come a long way in your learning and you have much to be grateful for.

You, after all, are the entire universe and when you began this series you thought you were a simple nothing. You have grown tremendously in awareness these last twelve school sessions and you have transformed a great deal just by believing what I have written. If you could see you from my perspective you would see a light that is beginning to outshine some of its surroundings. You are coming out of the dust and debris. In the beginning of this series I promised that I would pick you up and clean you off and put you gently back on your feet. I have said that God loves you and God is you and I have never deviated from the truth. You are being cleaned off and put oh so gently back on your feet. Now that you are getting there, I ask you to walk slowly so you do not slip and fall back into the mud and debris. Walk softly and walk in love.

꒰ঌ◈ কী꒱

*A*s you begin to change and grow as an individual, you will affect the whole. As you begin to raise your level of awareness, you will affect the whole. You will affect all who are near you and you will affect those you do not know. You will be adjusting to a particular level of consciousness and you will draw others into this consciousness just by opening the door. You are, in effect, becoming new thought and mixing it with old thought. This creates a new you that is mixed with the old you, and this also creates a new you that is able to accept greater change and greater awareness.

Then, as you add greater awareness, you become an even newer you. And this second you, who came from the old you, is mixed with this even newer you to create a brand new you. Next, of course, you begin to accept new thought again and this brand new you becomes a thing of the past as another even newer you springs to life. This is you un-layering you and becoming all that you can be. You will become all that you can be by simply allowing all to be possible. If you judge it you kill it! You cut off the flow of energy when you judge and it stifles all of creation. Stop judging you and you will continue to rejuvenate and reproduce your own self, to the extent that you become eternal beings as you are meant to be.

When you judge, you shut down the flow of energy or the juice of life. You deny existence to any given situation or creation. If you do not like it, allow it its place. Allow each situation to have a purpose and acknowledge that you simply may not be aware enough to see that purpose. Stop condemning everyone and everything out of your inability to see it clearly. When you get to another level of consciousness within your own self, you will begin to see many areas that you cannot see now. As you see these areas, you will begin to know how you misjudged them and distorted them in your past. I will save you this step. Stop judgment now and allow everything in creation to be. After all, when you get to the level of consciousness where you can see clearly that creation is all you, you will be happy you did not judge you, for you would have been cutting off life flow to you.

Now that you know you are the creator and the creation, you may use this information to achieve greater levels of awareness regarding how you live your lives. You may learn to create greater levels of consciousness, or you may learn how to create more of creation. You may even learn how to become peaceful and loving. Wouldn't that be nice? A peaceful loving God creating a peaceful loving world would be a wonderful gift for you to accept. Can you accept being peaceful and loving within yourself? Can you accept not judging yourself? Can you accept being a loving individual who is totally at peace within? When you can, you will reflect that peace outside of yourself also. You will see how no one is evil and no one is outside of you. You will see how you create a shadow, or reflection, for miles around you and you will see how it is a direct reflection of you.

Are you peace, love and harmony, or are you fear, chaos and revenge? Do you see peace, love and joy in all that you look upon, or do you see pain, hatred and terror? We must get you cleaned out. We must raise you out of your confusion and pain and lift you into joy and peace. It will not be as difficult as you believe. There has been great transformation already. A great deal of chaos has come to the surface and so has pain and fear. Once they arrive at the surface they can be seen for what they truly are and sent on to their proper place in creation. Law and order will be restored and so will the balance that has been temporarily disrupted. As you restore law and order you are really restoring trust and faith. Trust tells you that everything is going according to plan and faith allows you to keep that trust.

So now we have you wondering how long this process will take and I will tell you this much, it will not take as long to create peace as it took to create war and struggle. Peace will come very quickly compared to the descent into battle. The path to hell was a very slow one. The rise to heaven will be quite a fast shifting of consciousness. You will see for yourself. Many, many of you do see it for yourselves and it will not be too far in this near future. You will see the rise of certain types of behavior and you will know that many are shifting and changing their consciousness to create a shift in the consciousness of creation. Do you want to see it in your world? *Create it in you first and project it out into your world.* This is how you are God. You are the creator. You may change absolutely everything.

❧

You will begin to see how you are changing and you will begin to notice how this is all not as you had thought it would be. Man dreams from his own perspective and it is usually limited to a small point of view. God knows from a vast perspective and it is usually worked out for the benefit of the whole. Do not be afraid to heal in God's way. Do not be afraid to come forward into the light and acknowledge your fears and weaknesses. Your fears are simple energy that is trapped, and your weakness is pain induced. You are not going backward and becoming worthless, you are moving forward and becoming worthwhile.

You are a most incredible species and you are mutating into a more evolved version of your incredible self. As you begin to change into this new you who will change again into an even newer you, you will begin to take on new wisdom that tells you not to worry, that you are being processed and developed into a more versatile piece of you. You are being upgraded and moved into a more spiritually evolved you. You are being transformed and lifted up to become part of a new thought pattern that says, "All is good. All is God."

You will discover that, as you move into this new position of new awareness, your body may grind a bit with this shift. You may feel lag or you may feel sluggish or you may feel extreme exhaustion. This is the energy change affecting the tissues and the nervous system. This is also the cellular release of old programming to allow for new teaching and awareness. This is also emotional release, as all emotions of fear and hatred come to balance over the idea that not everything is as awful and horrible as was once believed (within the cells of the body). The body/mind is releasing and preparing for new shifts into new levels of awareness. As you experience these shifts you may also experience physical discomfort and twinges of sharp pain. This is due to the overload of pain that you have created for eons, and as you release it, it will make its presence known and felt.

You will find that as you begin to allow all pain and discomfort to leave you, you will become lighter and more aware than ever of your own cells and how you feel inside of you. Your emotions will give you an idea of how much stress and tension you have inside of you, and your verbal exchanges will show you how you are at this moment. You will protect and defend where you are at this moment and you will criticize and ridicule where you are going. This is a process of elimination. If you hear yourself condemning another for his or her lying ways, it is because you have been lied to and it caused you great confusion and pain. This criticism is your first clue that you are beginning to release all hold on pain and confusion, caused by some situation that was inflicted upon you by your own lies or the lies you were told. Watch what you criticize and judge, it will show you what you are going to be releasing.

As you become freer of your criticism and judgment, you will find that you are no longer attached to whether you are lied to or not. It was all built up pain, and stored anger from the past, that brought your rage and cynicism to the surface each time you caught your friend or lover lying to you. Now is a time for letting go of the lies, even the ones you have told yourself. It is also a time for letting go of all the pain that you carry concerning how you were treated as a child and in past lives. This is a great time of healing and understanding, and it is a great time for you. You are in celebration of the arrival of light within your own consciousness. You are receiving the light of love, the light of awareness, the light of healing, and you are growing in leaps and bounds.

You are just beginning to come into your own self and, as you arrive in all your glory and splendor, you will begin to feel a little cramped from all this debris that is carried from the past. You want to release it to make room for you and to allow space for more light. The light, after all, lifts you up and the light sets you free from the shadows of darkness. As you begin to feel your freedom, you will begin to know how good your life can be and how unafraid you will be to live to your fullest potential. Some of you believe you have been held back by your inability to create. No one is unable to create, as everyone is God and God creates. It is simply your fear of greater pain that holds you back, and once you release pain and its causes, you move forward with joy and lack of fear. Life becomes new again and you become part of it.

As you move into a more creative flow, it will be because you have left behind the blocks to your creative flow, which is your way of living life. Creation is living and all life evolves within and among itself. You are no longer simply the creator of all creation; you are living in and among your creation. You are creation just beginning to realize yourself. You have never experienced yourself as creation and now you are doing so. You are the one who projected into your own creation, to see how it would feel to take on what you made. You projected it out there and then you popped into your projection, to see how it would feel to be in it instead of outside of it watching it grow. You became the flower after you painted it on your huge canvas. You became the tree after you sketched it on your giant drawing board. Whatever you created, you then became it in order to experience it. You are the tree, you are the flower, you are the bear, you are the star, you are the rock and you are you.

❦

You have been very much a part of the coming of God. You are the created son of God. You are part of this plan to project God into all of creation. The son of God is simply an expression to show you how you came from God. You are part and parcel of the created whole. You are being pared down in order for you to become all that you can be. You are being moved into a new direction in order for you to become all that you will become.

As you move and as you grow, you will feel great changes within. You will find that you no longer need your anger to motivate you, and you will find that fear will be turned to understanding and will no longer be used as a catalyst to project you forward. Fear has been used to move you for so long that you have forgotten how to motivate from love. You will go on a diet and lose weight out of fear of losing a lover or fear of not getting a lover due to your size. You will be motivated to work to make money out of fear of being evicted or fear of not eating.

This fear also motivates you to marry someone you do not love. It is called fear of being alone.

You will find that as you begin to release these fears, you will begin to find new ways to motivate. You will use your own "desire to create" to build your new world. You each have creative desire and it is part of your genetic makeup. You are part of creation and the desire to be more of what you are is a natural part of your self-discovery. You will find that as you discover more and more of you; you are actually allowing more to exist. You are creating you by allowing you to show yourself. This is self-discovery and it is the unveiling of "all that is."

You will find that you are in this vast creative flow of energy and the more you discover parts of you, the more creation unfolds to greet you. You are twofold. You are becoming and you already *are*. You are beginning to wake up but that does not mean that you were not always here. You were and still are unconscious. The seeds were planted and the seeds sprouted into very nice stems or stalks. Now we must wait for the bud to bloom, to open up into a magnificent flower. You are this bloom that will open to show your true beauty and accept the gifts of creation. You are a flower in bloom and you are just now beginning to open. You have been in this process of growing for so long that you forgot the purpose was to grow large enough to finally bloom. Well, now you are large enough. Now is the springtime of your life and it is time to *open up* to the light.

You will not be kept in the dark any longer and you will literally be moved into position for this rise to ascension. You will find yourself in the heat of struggle when certain parts of you refuse to open, but open they will. You will become such a grand display of God's truth and love and strength. You will know all as it truly is and you will become aware of many things that you have kept from yourself.

You are a magnificent being of light and you are just now beginning to share your true identity with yourself and with others. As this new level of consciousness appears and you begin to understand your role in all of creation, you will begin to understand that not everyone is in this for the long run. Some are only here to play a short-term role and to assist those who are in this transformation process. They know their role and they do not wish to play your role, or they would have come into this dimension as you. Since you are you and they are themselves, I highly suggest that you encourage them to follow their own instincts and play their own role (whatever that may be).

Now is the time of great awakening and a great seeking of truth. As you move among your own creation, I wish you to remember that you too have your role to play. You too wish to explore the depths of your own creation by becoming all that you are. If someone does not wish to hear it, do not force it on them. Your truth is your truth. They have their own script for their own role in all of this. Sometimes they know, better than you, what is going on in their reality and their own creation.

You will find that as you move into perspective, you will be seeing *all* as acceptable and tolerable. You will find that you have a new tolerance and acceptance for life, and even a new appreciation for life. This, of course, will lead to a whole new self-appreciation that will be expressed by you in many ways. You will find that the more you appreciate you the more you like you, and the more you like you the greater the possibility of falling in love with you. Then we will have our desired results; you loving you once again, you being all that you can be, and you above all else in your life.

This is how we put you back on top. This is how we save you from the depths of despair and the pits of confusion. No more depths and no more pits and no more big holes for you to fall into. You are rising up out of despair and right into the arms of God and love. This is being done by you and for you, and it is glorious to behold. You wish to rush into the arms of your Creator and say, "Thank you for loving me enough to enter me." And your Creator will look upon you with great love and say, "Yes, I created you so I could be you." And you will then know that you have been both created and creator, and you will love all that this entails. For now I bid you Godspeed on your path to you!

❧

You have come to a point in your evolution that tells you to be who you are, only you have changed and grown to the extent that you don't know who you are. As you begin to realize how everyone and everything is you,

you will begin to realize how you are simply viewing the many possibilities of your own identity. You can be anything and you can see any and all views of you. As you begin to look into you and see all the different perspectives that allow you to be "all that is," you will find yourself a little confused by the vastness of your being and the vastness of your choices.

You are not discovering all parts of you in order to harm you. You are simply bringing all parts of you to the surface so that you might see where your fears lie. As you bring your fears to the surface, you begin to feel vulnerable and insecure. This is due to the fact that your fear is the only thing that tells you, "You are in danger or unsafe." When your fear says, "Danger, this is bad," you may have triggered a big fear that you do not wish to look at. This fear was triggered so you might be allowed to grow above this fear and to know that nothing is dangerous in God's reality.

So; as you struggle with your fears you begin to know how it feels to not be well received. You see, fear says, "No you can't; this is unsafe." God says, "Yes, you can, for all life is safe." Your fear will tell you to say you are sorry and your fear will tell you to say you are wrong. Now, the interesting part here is that you can be sorry and not know that you are, or you can feel great shame and not know that you do. Often your shame is holding you back, and it creates a wide variety of instances to allow you to feel shameful or unworthy. As your shame creates for you (remember there are many parts of you at work here), you will feel less than worthy.

You are now in this position of feeling less than worthy and it offends you, because it says that you do not deserve. As you begin to sink lower into your unworthy feelings, fear will begin to abate, as he believes you have heeded his warning that there was danger and that you have been put back in a safe position, which to fear is "locked behind a wall of fear." As you create more and more situations that call for your fear to rise to the surface and warn you, I wish you to stay calm and move ahead as though nothing has happened. This will tell fear that you know better than he and that there really is nothing to fear. As fear begins to see how you are moving ahead, he will be confused and he will look for a new place to live, as fear can only live where he can feed off of another. When you no longer feed him your energy he goes to a better place, where he can receive the energy to grow big and strong. Stop feeding fear and he will shrivel up and disappear.

You are moving into an entirely new area that will be "living in the light with no fear of the future." This era will be very conducive to your worthiness and your kind loving spirit. As you move forward without the restraints of fear, you will find that you are moving forward into love and away from the chains of fear that have bound you. You are moving ahead and as you do so you will leave a great deal behind you. Most of what you leave will be huge parts of you that were transformed into fear. You are leaving the darkness and it will be very soon that you begin to walk in the light and know the true meaning of love.

≈⁂≈

*F*or as long as you have been "becoming," you have been unable to see how you create and how you belong to your creation. Now I am going to show you how you exist as both your creation and you, the creator. Most often you begin to have an idea or thought. This idea or thought begins to unfold into awareness and is then sent out as energy. As this idea or thought is run through you as energy, it becomes part of your genetic makeup. It literally becomes you. If the idea is a fun and healthy idea it may create some good health and entertainment in your life. But, what if the idea was a frightening one? What if it was based on a thought that said, "You are not good. You did a bad thing?"

If you begin to look closely at your genetic makeup, you will find that you have many of these genetic thoughts that have hardened into your life support system. You have many layers within you that all carry information concerning every aspect of life and death and love and prosperity, and even which food to eat or not eat. You have a multi-layered system within you that is loaded with genetically coded information, and this is what you are. You are what you think. You are this coded information you carry.

So now we have this idea or thought and it says, "I am bad, I do not deserve." This, of course, is connected to being bad, as "not deserving" is taught to be a punishment.

When you are bad you lose a toy, or get your television privileges revoked, or lose your allowance for a week. So, you already have the programming in place that taught you to "punish if bad." Now you are thinking about how bad you were, or are, and this part of you, who taught you about punishment, is ready to do its duty and create whatever punishment is necessary to fit the degree of badness that you are now being. Once you learn that you are not bad, nor are you stupid, nor are you ugly, you will no longer activate this center within you that punishes you for being un-perfect. You will also begin to see how, as you begin to think yourself good and loving and lovable, you begin to change the genetic buildup within you that was based on the old *idea* that you are bad.

All of the old programming will then *shift* to accommodate this new thought, which is now moving in and taking its rightful place as part of you. Thought and belief make you up. They are what you are. Release the damaging thoughts and allow the good healing thoughts. Know how you judge you and criticize you, so that you can erase that part of your behavior. You are constantly creating you as you go and you can literally create a brand new you with a brand new set of codes and a brand new clear awareness.

Each code within each cell is part of you and therefore affects all of you. If you have a code that is in you and you wish it weren't, you have no way to change it unless you can access it. You must know it. You must see it in order to know that it is there. If you do not look at it, you have no way to repair the damage and change the code.

It would be like a blindfolded plumber or electrician doing his job. How far do you think he would get in finding and repairing the problem? He would probably trip and fall flat on his face before he even made it to the object to be repaired.

This is you. I bring it to the surface so you can fix it, by first looking and knowing it was in you in the first place. You then say, "Oh God, I hate when this happens, or that happens." And this is your first clue that there is damage that must be fixed. If it feels good and you enjoy it, it is okay to keep. If it feels uncomfortable, you will want to do some new coding to set things straight within the cellular walls. This new coding can be done by replacing the old idea or thought that is stuck in you with a new idea or thought.

The best thing to do is to use neutrality. If the damaging thought is, "Oh no, this is bad, it always happens to me," replace it with "I am good and all good things happen for me." This way you are not pushing and struggling to change the old thought, you are simply adding to it. If you were to program, "I am good and this old thought is wrong and will cause me harm," you will be creating greater conflict and a struggle to accept one thought as good and one as bad. Do not make anyone or anything bad, not even your own thoughts. This will allow for total acceptance of all.

Now; as you begin to recode your inner workings, this will be reflected in your outer reality or the reflection of your world. You will begin to see shifts and changes. In the beginning, you may see all of the old programming that is being brought to the surface for you to see and repair. After you get yourself all tuned up, you may begin to see some pretty surprising results. You may even begin to create a loving world for your reality. Each time that you reprogram an idea or thought, you literally affect the entire world. Keep your thoughts simple and know that love is number one. Not romantic sexual love, but the simple knowingness that allows for everything to be part of creation

As you move forward with less and less negative programming, you will find yourself enjoying the flow of your life. You will no longer be punishing you because you will have changed that simple little cellular memory that said, "When I am bad, I must lose something or be hurt." Once you lose this idea, or thought, and replace it with, "I am good and all good is mine," you will feel much better about your life and how you are creating it.

You are not part of a failing system; you are part of a changing system. Know that, as this system of yours changes, you will draw to you the new changes. All is complete when it goes out and comes back. And everything that comes to you came from you to begin with. It all begins and ends with you. You are the sender and the receiver. You are the creator and the created. You are the whole circuit and you are "all that is." It all runs through you, and in you, and around you, and out, and back in again. You are this giant electrical circuit and you have no idea how magnificent you are.

࿊

*A*s I begin to walk this planet, I do believe I will enjoy being fully in your shoes. It is most important to remember that this shift is simply God arriving in you. It is God becoming part of your daily life and you becoming aware that you are God and God is you. As you shift into a greater degree of consciousness you will be capable of feeling more and more. As you feel more and more, you become more sensitive to what is occurring and how to move with it. You will find that you move easily enough when you are in control, and now it is time to learn to move when you are not in control. Most of you freeze up when you are not in control because your fear of losing control is so great.

This is the time for losing control! You will see this occur to many people in many different ways. Do not be frightened when you see those who are losing control. Do not be concerned that everything has gone wrong and will never come into balance. Some of you are simply time bombs of hatred and fear. It is not necessary to get involved in someone else's clearing and balancing. If they are losing control it is good. It is not awful, or bad, or horrible. It only looks like that to you because your point of view is focused on good vs. bad.

The awfulness of creation is your favorite focus. You love to find the horror and the wrong. You love your gossip shows that exploit tragedy and unfair play. You love to be involved in a good "whodunit" novel or a good "horror" show. It's what excites you and now it's what excites your children. It gets your blood moving and it thrills you. You love the chase to find and capture the bad guy and you love the thrill of a good fight scene. This is what you have created in your world without consciously knowing that you have.

You are now in a place of great change, and with it will come a shift in the reception of violence and anger. As you begin to shift and clear your violence and anger, you will see others doing the same. It is not necessary to concern yourself with others. You have enough to do right here inside of you. You will find that others will walk their own path and do just fine without you, regardless of what you think. Others are here for a purpose, just as you are, and they do not need you to tell them what that purpose is or how to continue to grow into God. You don't exactly have an inside track on this becoming God business, so I suggest you allow God to be and do as he sees fit.

When you begin to allow others the space that is required to clear and balance, you will find that you do not mind so much after all. You do not really care as long as you are still allowed to do what you wish to do. As a matter of fact, all of your fears are connected to the loss of your ability to do what you want to do. There is really no other fear. You begin to fear others who might be losing control and going on a rampage only because it may affect you and your life, or someone you are so attached to that it feels like your life.

This is the basis of all fear. Being next to get hurt, or being next to get robbed, or being next to die, or being next to lose! Losing is the bottom line because, in loss, you believe you will not get to do what you want. Your dreams will no longer come true because you pictured your life this way and not that way. You pictured your life full of love and with all the people you care about, and when someone you care about is killed you get a big jolt and your whole dream is shattered. Or, you may be attached to the person who might attack and kill others. In this case, your dream is still shattered because you did not plan on this. You did not dream of a future with a loved one who was to grow into a killer.

So now you must pick up the pieces, as you say, and move on with your life. All of these pieces that you must pick up are parts of your dream that you still wish to keep. You will find that as you put these pieces back together again and create a new dream, it may shatter again at the next loss. The only reason your dream shatters is because it is held in place by control. You control your dream. If your dream was flexible and you had no need to control, you would see how it would automatically *shift* to handle and accommodate any disaster. This shifting is a natural part of the flow of consciousness. You, however, in your unaware state, have blocked consciousness in order to stay unconscious.

As you begin to unblock consciousness, you will have a greater tolerance for "all that occurs." You will also know more of you than you have ever known before, and, in the knowing of you, will come the release of the grip you have on your reality in order to control. You will find that even you are losing control and this is good.

❧

*W*e will now discuss the proper way to "be." The proper way to "be" is to always show kindness to yourself. You must learn kindness and come away from anger. Kindness is a softness that allows you to treat yourself gently and without harsh words or thoughts. When you are being kind to you, you do not think "Oh shit, I am so damn stupid, look what I just did wrong." When you are kind to yourself your thought will be, "Wow this didn't work out, I wonder why, or what is next." Do you see the difference in the effect that your thoughts may have upon your own physical form? If you constantly chastise yourself, you will eventually shrink away from your own self. You will move away in order to get relief from the anger that you are forever projecting at you.

You are now in a position to be kind and loving to yourself, and, once you learn to love yourself without judgment, you will be capable of loving all without judgment. You are not here to beat yourself up; you are here to love yourself. You are here to realize the potential of created harmony and you are here to show God his own self. How can you reflect back to God what he is if you cannot accept what you are? How can you show God his own creation if you hate being the creation? How can you judge what you do not understand and how can you not love what you are? These are the questions that keep you at odds within yourself. Part of you wants to accept you and to know that you are just fine and everything is going according to plan. But another part wants to run for its life, because it is not in control and therefore it is frightened, because it believes it will never be in control and therefore it will always lose.

You do not always lose; you only believe that you do. You are not in a position to see how you are actually winning. Once you are moved to a greater level of awareness, you will see how you do not lose, not ever. You will see how you are only in a state of confusion and how your perception was and still is a little out of balance. Well, okay! A lot out off balance. But the good news is, you are now arriving in time to clear this mess that has been created and you will have everything flowing smoothly in no time.

This is the time for you to know that you are wonderful and good. This is a time for you to know that, through simple misperception, you made of few decisions about what was awful or distasteful to you, and now you will learn that it was not as you *thought*.

I will now tell you a story. Once upon a time you were walking down the street and a fat old man jumped out of the bushes and frightened you. He was dirty and unshaven and he smelt like garbage. His weight fell on you and crushed you to the sidewalk. He then began to flail his arms madly about your head and he is screaming obscenities at you. Next thing you know, your clothes are being torn and you become quite enraged and frightened and panicked. Now he pushes you down face first into the cement and your nose begins to bleed. You now see blood and know that something awful is about to happen. About this time, he pulls himself up and runs like hell as you begin to shout, "Help, stop him. He attacked me!"

The moral of this story is: this man fell off the second floor as he was watering his plants. He is blind and did not know where he landed or how to get up and back to his safe home. He had no intention of attacking anyone and he only pushed your face into the cement because he was so terrified and out of control with fear. There have been many instances in your life that have been perceived as truly awful, so now you always expect awful to occur. Let go of awful and watch for the good. Know that if one thing goes wrong another is on the way. Know that you are not in control and know that you are learning to become God by allowing God to become you.

☙❧

You will find that as you begin to rise above the dense belief that you are inherently bad, you will find that you are truly good. You will find that the belief in bad is centered around a great need for punishment. This need for punishment usually comes from deep within the soul at a more inherited level. Some parts of you are inherited from those who came before. Just as your children will inherit an earth after you finish with it, you have inherited many aspects within your own being. This is not to say that you have been the victim of this inheritance. You knew full well what you were walking into and you still came.

Now is a very important time upon this plane. You are finding that you are growing as unique individuals as never before. You are all separating and multiplying and separating and multiplying and separating... well, you get the idea. So now you are all so separated that you can't recall how you got here or why you came. You have little to no recall of your mission, and you not only don't remember who you are, but you also don't remember who your neighbors are.

This is the time for returning to awareness and it is a time of exposing secrets and it is the time of being open and allowing the truth to come forward. You are moving into an area that is new to you and this area is love. Love will allow you to walk your path with little irritation and not much in the way of distraction.

You will find that as you let go of the need for punishment, that was inherited by you from past travelers to this plane, you will rise quickly to the position of awareness that will assist you up and out of denial and darkness. You are rising rapidly and you will find that only what you project will be yours and what others project will be theirs. You need not get involved with saving others if you do not wish to. I know you are taught to put others before yourself but this does not work. Why? It is not possible to save another. You are *in* you and it is only possible for you to be your own personal savior. The others live in their bodies with their soul and their guidance and you live in you. Stay in your own house and clean your own floors. I do not expect to see you over at your neighbor's house cleaning his or her floors when you are still not ascended.

Light your own fire. Teach your own self. Stir your own heart, and fan your own flame. You drive your car and let everyone else drive theirs. Yes, some are still learning to drive as you are. Yes, some may have an accident here or there and yes, some will even die, or leave from these accidents. However, you and I both know that there are no accidents, so we'd best allow whatever is planned to unfold.

Do not be so afraid to 'not' help! You have been told that you must help if you are to be a good person. Most of you don't know how to help and you only compound an already explosive situation. It is best to stay in your own yard and not run your neighbor's life until you have unraveled your own. This is the most important time for understanding, and you must be willing to see all from a new perspective in order to gain insight, which will lead you to understand why you are here. Once you understand why you are here you may gain some insight into why your neighbor is here and what his or her life is about. Until that time, I wish you would give up your *need* to be a do-gooder and give it a rest! Leave everything to God. He's not really as incompetent and irresponsible as you seem to think.

❧❧

As you begin to see the benefits of becoming whole and aware, you will begin to see how you have always been fragmented and broken into parts. You have separated to a degree that is most unusual. It has come to the attention of this world that you no longer know who you are or where you have come from. It also has come to the attention of this world that part of you is missing and not engaged. This part of you that is missing is in a state of dormancy and is about to come awake and learn to grow. As this part of you comes awake, you will have a real surprise. You will be wondering how you could be so unaware of this part that has always been you, but not noticed by you.

You will find that you not only do not recognize parts of you, you also deny parts of you. You do not wish to belong to, or take responsibility for many parts of you that are less than what you consider to be good. As these parts of you begin to surface and make themselves known, you will be surprised at how much of you was, and is, hidden from your awareness. This is not some sneaky plot to avoid detection. This is simply your time to wake up to who you are and how vast you are. You are multi-dimensional and multi-focused and multi-leveled. You have many layers and many plots and plans programmed into you. These are hereditary as well as accumulated through choice.

You have many levels of you that have not yet touched the surface. As these levels come to light you will expand to accept this new part of you. As you accept more and more of you, you allow for the entrance of more of you. You allow for the expansion and growth. This is the time of growing inward and expanding inward. The time for outer expansion is over. It is as though you are a giant cell who is breathing, first in and then out. You are growing the part of you that is deep inside of you. As this part grows and develops, it will allow you to become more of "all that is." You actually are "all that is," but you are just now waking to the fact that you are.

As you walk this planet in total darkness and confusion, you begin to stumble and fall because you cannot see the stumbling blocks that are ahead. As you walk this planet in love and light, you will see with clarity and know where you are going and what to avoid in order to assure prompt arrival. You will become clear by allowing all parts of you to be shown to you, so that you might be acceptable to your own self. Once you are acceptable to your own self, you begin to move to a new level that will allow more of you to become acceptable. You cannot talk a child into looking under the bed if the child is convinced beyond a doubt that a monster is waiting under his or her bed to kill him/her. It is all part of this process you are going through. You do not wish to look at certain parts of you because they are illusionary monsters in your mind.

As you let go of this need to hide from the monsters and you begin to come out and face your fears, it will change your entire reality to the extent that you will allow fear to move out of you and awareness to move in. You will become so full of wisdom that you will wish for only more wisdom at whatever cost. Nothing will frighten you and nothing will lead you astray. You will know that it is all you and that if you fear you, you will never get to know all of you. There really is nothing to fear. It is all part of you and it is all made up of you and your choices of long ago. You are waking up to the part of you who has a new level of understanding to share with you. This part will guide you into the less conscious and more fearful parts. It is you helping you. It is you opening up to receive you. It is time.

⁂

*A*s you begin your ascent into the higher realms of consciousness, you may find that your body shifts into a higher vibration in order to accommodate your rise. This could cause some temporary discomfort, just as you may lose your hearing temporarily when you fly in a jet. It is all part of the body/soul adjustments and I do not wish you to become overly concerned. In some cases you may see great changes and in others only slight changes. This is all part of this process and it will come and go until you have balanced at your new vibration. Bodywork or massage can be very helpful in such cases, and will assist your body in connecting with your soul in this attempt to rise up.

As you begin this shift, you may begin to see many other changes take place in your physical form. Many of these changes may feel like aging or even illness. As you all know, illness is simply discomfort from beliefs which are too painful and aging is simply a symptom of illness. All of these symptoms are only a sign that change is occurring. In the same way that change brings awareness, change can also bring healing. As you begin to realize that you are releasing old programming, and it is this old idea of death and a need for punishment that is causing a shift in your physical well-being as it goes, you will be aware that this is simply how you release and clear the old ideas and thoughts.

You are now in a very important position, that of healer and that of healed. You are healing you and becoming healed. You are growing beyond limitation and you are learning to see where you were and how far you have come. You are being put in a position that might accommodate and even support your search for truth. As you move ahead you are not only supported, you are loved. You are accepted and tolerated and cherished. You are doing wonderful work and you are greatly appreciated for your assistance in this healing of the world of creation. You are part of a much bigger picture and you are literally preparing your own way. You are taking responsibility for you and you are making you well.

You have come to a point that is your turning point. You are turning you around and facing you in a new direction. This direction is toward the light of awareness. This direction is toward the light of love. This direction is toward the light of forgiveness and this direction is toward the movement of your own soul. You are raising you up. You are allowing your soul to shift to a high enough level of comprehension that it may assist its own self in the rising of this soul above the illusion of this dense plane. You are shifting and your body is shifting and moving with you. You are rising up and you need not push aside your body to do so. Your body is yours to command and it will respond to your truth as it always has.

As you move further and further ahead you will discover that you are not only moving, you are moving upward and inward. You are shifting and taking all parts of you with you and your body will believe what your soul is allowed to show it. You will rise faster and faster, as your body becomes more and more accustomed to these shifts in consciousness that allow for this shift in the body, that allows for the rise to new levels of total acceptance, and the ultimate goal which, of course, is "heaven on earth."

❧

You are moving into an area that is mostly off limits to you. You have never explored this area before and when you do, I wish you to remember that it is not to be judged. Allow all parts of you to do the work you came to do. Allow all parts of you to unfold before you and you will begin to see how you work in conjunction with other parts.

Not only do you work in conjunction with other parts, you also work around issues that other parts have control over. You surround yourself with information regarding the care and maintenance of you, and then you move into a more appropriate way of seeing how this care and maintenance shall evolve.

You may start by wishing you felt better or happier, and the next thing you know you are beginning to change in order to accommodate this wish or idea. Then you begin to see that you have others at work in you and you begin to realize how there is more to you than what meets the eye. As you continue to discover new parts of yourself and how they feel, you begin a journey of sorts. This is a journey within and it will take you through you and into your depths. As this journey progresses, you begin to realize how you are not only not happy, but you are miserable. This, of course, is after you have journeyed into that part of you that holds misery.

Now you begin to move on to other areas within you and you begin to see how you are not only miserable, you are also afraid and insecure. As you roam around within these feelings, you begin to realize that, on the surface, you are not yet in touch with these feelings. These feelings are at a very deep level and you do not yet have access to them. They are very big and very overwhelming. So you move into and out of these feelings and try to explore without too much interference. Then you begin to move into another area where you see pain. This pain is red-hot to look at and it is very, very split. It is fragmented into various parts and it is so hot you must move very cautiously around it.

You have come to this pain and now you wish to discover its origin. It is not simply a part of you; it is feeding off you as a fire would feed off the house it is burning. You are very intrigued by this red-hot pain and you circle it cautiously to explore its connection to you. You then begin to see where it is moving from and you trace it back; back into you, back into your history. You find this pain attached to many parts of you and it is a multi-level pain that began as sparks that were ignited by many small events that were charged with energy or negative response. These charges set off this fire that burns in you and these charges are carried in your electrical circuit system. They are alive in you and they are in the negatively and positively charged ions that float around in you.

You have set yourself on fire by your own charge. You have heated and sparked to the extent that you are a live wire that is untouchable, because you are so hot that you are ready to melt down your own body. You are practically on fire with your own pain and electrical charges, and this is why you hurt and feel shame and want to be held gently and loved. You want love so badly that you try again and again to capture the least little kindness or thoughtfulness toward you and call it love. The love of you is twofold. It is being centered in you and it is being centered in love. You do not require a date or a lovemaking session or even to be held. You do require a neutralizing within you to bring you back into balance. You require an enema daily to release the negatively and positively charged ions that roam within you and heat up enough to ignite small fires, that turn into little irritations and then grow into bigger eruptions, that end in towering infernos right here inside of you.

You are on fire and we are putting you out. Water is good for putting out fire. Drink it and clean your bowels with it. It will soothe you. It will calm you and it will cool you down. You may then continue to explore within you without getting burnt. You are moving into unknown territory, and the more your fires rage the greater chance that you will have some unpleasant experience while going within. This is simply part of the process and if you hear horror stories about someone who channeled and released an uncontrollable monster, it is simply their fire burning out of control and the meltdown occurring on the surface. There are many who have big fires raging within, and they too will learn how they are becoming God. It is not necessary for you to point out to them what is occurring for they have their own teacher and guide.

Each of you is encoded with your own teacher and guide. This teacher knows what will work for the individual self, as this teacher *is* the individual self. Allow others to see their own teacher and to drive their own car (body). You are busy driving yours and no one cares for a backseat driver to tell them how well they are doing or how lost they might be. Everyone is on the right road and everyone is God growing from seed. And everyone has their own fires to put out.

୬ୱଈ

*Y*ou will find that you no longer have a need to punish you when you finally give up the programming that said "you are bad." As you let go of this need that has always been at work in you and has always created punishing situations for you, you will begin to flow into the goodness of life. You will begin to receive without blocks and you will begin to enter an entirely new era of self-respect and self-love. You will find that as you enter this new era, you will be much at ease and much relaxed and greatly appreciated by you. You will probably become greatly appreciated by others also, since what you do for you is reflected out and then received back.

As you grow in this new self appreciation, you will begin to grow in a truly new direction. The old you has always said, "Put me down, hurt me and keep me in my place so I don't get too frightened by my own actions." This old you was taught to restrain the self at all costs and to keep rules and laws to govern the self, because the self cannot be trusted. The self was thought to be dangerous to its own creation. The self was thought to be too frightening and the self was thought to be too much to take all at once. Now the self is being guided by spirit and spirit is in the driver's seat. Now the self has purpose and a destination, and now the self has trust and faith and the knowledge that is not alone.

The self is beginning to establish a whole new "idea" of its own self. It is beginning to create out of direction with some clarity, instead of out of command with little or no foresight. It will be wonderful to see your own self become all that you can be. It will be part of the growth and development of the Spirit of God. You are becoming God by allowing God to call the shots and by taking ego out of your driver's seat. Ego did what he was taught, and was in a position of control, and will not wish to retire quickly without a plan for his retirement. Ego will move on to replace fear and develop a new way of viewing and handling fearful situations.

Ego will still be with you, his job will simply change. He will retire from judgment of right and wrong, and he will become more of a mediator between your faculties to decipher between your various choices. As he takes on this new role he will become very happy, as he will no longer be in charge of destroying and punishing you. He never really wanted that job, but he was pushed into the position by the creation of judgment and he was in position and had little to say about his role. Now he will be happy and have less turmoil.

When you begin to lose your grip on reality as you now know it, you will be moving forward into a reality that is "too much of a good thing" for some of you. Since you are not accustomed to having "too much of a good thing" in your lives, you may find your new reality a little difficult to accept at first. And you may try to revert to the old way, which is to punish and take away from the self in order to keep control over all parts that believe (ultimately) that they can fly and do whatever they want, as they know how powerful they are.

You see, this entire tying down of you was done out of fear that you would, and could, rise up and take over. You have the power and the ability to be anything and to do anything. It was thought best to develop slowly and give the illusion of entrapment, in order to keep you down on earth until you could learn to stay down on your own. It was necessary first to learn to stay down. You all knew how to ascend and how to zap here and zig or zag over there. The problem in the beginning was keeping you in place long enough to get you to grow into matter.

Well, now you are in place and thoroughly stuck in matter. You are so static that now you don't want to get up out of it and fly. You got grounded and now you think that your wings have been clipped or that you never had wings in the first place. You do have wings! You are all angels! You are the ones who came here to discover and you got stuck and never returned.

Now it is time to return and to know that you are free to fly and have always been. The message was sent out to stay put and you stayed, in the only way you could at that time. The message to stay put is now being removed and you are now being told to rise up. This is all coming out of your central nervous system which literally has the ability to paralyze you and keep you in place. You are now removing this command and replacing it with a new one that says, "Rise up and know who you are." It will take a little time for the cobwebs of hypnosis to leave you enough so that you clearly remember how to fly, but it will be in due time and with your approval.

Now is the time of the beginning and the end. It is the end of the world as you once knew it and the beginning of a whole new you. You will soar and you will fly to new heights. It is not the beginning of death and destruction; it is the beginning of love, peace and wisdom. It is the beginning of truth and the putting aside of fiction. You are no longer in need of the lies you have used to keep you hypnotized and frozen in position. Now is a time of great power and even greater glory. This is the beginning of God!

❧

You will ultimately discover that you are so in need of change that change will become your only alternative. You will find that as you seek to become free of the limitations of your third dimensional experience, you wonder how you ever got so bound up in the first place. You are very much in need of unbinding and flowing. You are very much in need of growing and expanding your intelligence. As you grow in proportion to your wisdom you may then expand and take on more of you or more of your own intelligence.

Most of what is described in your world as intelligence is actually learned information. I am speaking now from a level of awareness and experience. Wisdom and intelligence are actually very similar. One is wise and one is knowing. As you learn to be wise and to know, you will see advantages to change that you did not know existed. You are in direct proportion with your level of awareness and you operate from that level. If you have little to no awareness you can only operate on little to no awareness. If, however, you have expanded awareness you may begin to operate from expanded consciousness.

Once you develop this type of expanded awareness, your field of vision improves and you can literally see into a future possibility. This is done through awareness and with the option of intelligence to direction. Once you learn to use your awareness, you will become very much a part of who you are by the simple act of being aware of who you are. It is not good for you to do harm to you unless your intent is harm. It is best to avoid harm and direct conflict unless your intent is harm and conflict. You must learn how you react and overreact and then find out why. You are not responding from love and you are not responding from a true sense of self when you begin to feel attacked and cheated.

You are beginning to move into a new level of awareness, and it will evaporate much of your confusion and it will bring you into a new sense of self. You will begin to know that you have the ability to know what you create and exactly how you created it. It will also show you that you do not belong to others, you belong to you. You belong to God and you do not know how to belong without God showing you the way. As you move about in your awareness, you will begin to understand the true meaning of expansion. Your awareness moves and shifts as you look at it. It grows as you grow and it moves over here as you move over here. You take your awareness with you and you learn how to know from truth and not from lessons.

A lesson will tell you to not touch a hot flame. If you burn your fingers enough times you will stop touching the flame. This is conditioning, this is not awareness. It is learning through a painful experience. But, what drove you to the curiosity and examination of the flame in the first place? And why did you touch it repeatedly? Awareness will tell you that you thought it was home. You were drawn to the flame because it is light and light feels like home. You touched it repeatedly because you wanted a way in so badly. You are not touching it to learn not to touch a flame. You are touching it to learn how to get into it without pain.

This is you. You are all trying to get into the light without pain and pain is what you have used for eons to condition yourselves, so pain is what you are now using to un-condition yourselves. You will soon learn that no matter what, you will always be drawn to the light.

❧

*I*t is now time to decide if you wish to create your world for you or if you wish to create for others. The most important part of creating is to be who you are and to do it for you. You are now learning that you are in this to learn to become you, so you might as well learn how to enjoy being you. You are a very fine person and you need not explain yourself to anyone. You will find that as you begin to develop into more and more of yourself you will no longer be anyone else. When you try to please others you will learn that you are just as important as they are. You are also just as needy and this is why you ultimately try to please them. You are not to be so hard on you. Allow everyone to be who they are and you will learn to be who you are.

As you begin to learn to be who you are, you will become all that is necessary for your development as God. You will see how you no longer require the use of words to negotiate or to put your point across. You will simply learn to think your way clear and to rise above constant negotiation or communication on a verbal level.

Communication can be a very good thing; however, you don't always communicate what you really think. It is not necessary to communicate your views and your reasons. Allow for interpretation, as you will always have a gap in what is said versus what is accepted or heard. Often you do not hear what is said to you. It becomes very threatening on some level and you get all upset and begin to think that this or that is being said. The most important thing to remember is that you will always be communicating to a projection and this projection can only receive what you are allowing it to receive. You have projected this image to show you how confused you are; and this image is confused as that is what you projected.

When you begin to rise above your own projected fear and pain, you will begin to send out new projections that will be much simpler and less confusing. Most of your simpler and less confusing examples of projection have not yet arrived as you are not exactly the exemplification of simplicity. You will find that as you become less and less confusing, you will become more and more peaceful. This type of peace will come from knowing who you are and knowing that everything is safe.

You are now moving into an area that is not so hot as some of the past explosive areas. This area is that of honesty and knowing what honesty is. Honesty is not giving the self away; it is simply being all that you are without worry about how you appear. As you learn to be honest with yourself you will learn to be you. As you learn to be you, you learn to become more of you. The more of you that you become, the less of you that has to be left outside of you. You are this big you who does not allow all of you to be seen out of fear that all of you is not good enough. You will find that as you allow all of you to be seen you will be almost as big as I am. Actually, you will be as big as I am, as all that you are is me and all that I am is you.

You are not here to be cheated out of part of you. You are here to be the biggest you that there is – which is all of you, which is "all that is." You are moving and growing and evolving into "all that is" and you will learn to know who you are without learning to overthrow your own efforts. The best way to learn about you, without negating you, is to allow everything to be as is. Stop trying to override or overturn what takes place and simply move on to the next thing and let go of any current conflict. The more you stay in a conflict, the greater your ability to stay in conflicts becomes. The faster you move out of conflict and into peace the faster you get peace. The faster you get peace the more quickly you receive joy.

Act as if each conflict will open the door to peace. Do not confuse conflict with emotional instability. That, in itself, is another area. As you resolve your conflict you will move over to see how easily conflicts can simply be avoided. It basically takes two opposing views or two opposing polarities to create conflict. Don't allow this to distract you because you know that all views exist, therefore, all views are legitimate and acceptable. Therefore, you need never push your point of view on another.

As you learn to forgo conflict and rise above it to a state of projected peace, you will find that you no longer care to be in conflict, or even to convince another how you see it or how you feel it. You do feel it as well as see it you know? You feel out situations and this is how you trust or do not trust. Does it feel okay or does it feel unstable? This is how your gut feeling works, you begin to feel something amiss and you begin to try to figure out what is being said, or not said, to prevent honesty from entering a given situation. You are usually all in a state of confusion and do not know what you are projecting outward, so you do not always accept what has been received and then returned to you.

You are mostly learning to be who you are and to see how you have developed and to see how you have learned, and to show you how you do not wish to be in conflict any longer. You are learning to rise above conflict and let it go. You are not learning how to fight to the bitter end as you already know how to do that. And you are not learning to get the last word in as you already know how to do that. You are simply learning to let go of conflict and of being right. It is okay to let go and not be the winner. It is okay to let go and walk away or even run away. It is okay to not be a warrior. You are an angel of peace not a soldier of war. That is, of course, unless you choose to be the warrior and forgo the angel role. It's your choice and you get to live with all of your choices.

◈

We are now moving into an area that will be known as non-eternal. This area is part of what is considered to be dead. There are parts of you that you believed to be dead and to be non-effective. These parts are not dead. You have simply shut them down. As you learn to reopen certain parts of you, you will learn to reopen your own psyche. This will allow you to see more and to know more. You will be allowed to be all that you can be without interfering with your own creative ability. It is as if we are tuning you up within your own self and we are teaching you how to operate all parts of you.

You are going to find that this probing and tweaking will cause some body parts to send certain signals out of fear of not being balanced. You see, the body believes that it is working perfectly now in its unbalanced state. This is due to the fact that it is not accustomed to ever having been balanced. It is only part of this big body that is called creation and it has always been out of balance and off-center. So now that you are bringing it back into balance, you are very much in distress. The body believes it is actually going out of balance when, in actuality, it is returning to perfect balance. Of course, since the body has never attained perfect balance, it is simply confused as to where it is going and what will occur.

So; you may receive signals that allow you to rise above certain situations only to be pulled down by body's inability to follow thought. Body has been programmed for so long to be down that it finds itself fighting the rise up. You will see that body is no longer working for you, but has decided that it knows best. At these times, allow your body to rest and to have its own way. Allow your body to recuperate before you begin to push it into ascension mode once again. It will work best for you if you work with it. You must learn to understand that you are not all there is of you. You have so many parts of you that you do not know exist, and you have so many parts of you that have not yet shown themselves to other parts of you. They are all within you and they all have a role to play.

As you learn to develop your ability to see into yourself, you will be seeing parts that are just now showing themselves to you. They have always been you, but you did not know they existed as part of you. And you certainly did not know that they were pushing your buttons and making you dance to their tune. You have always drawn to you those who will become enamored with you for short periods of time, out of a need to fulfill themselves. As these enamored ones finish feeding or fulfilling themselves by your emotional support, or financial support, or psychic support, they become full and wish to move on. Sometimes they will return to feed some more and sometimes they never return.

You also feed off of others in this same fashion. You will be drawn to one who can give you moral support or financial support or emotional support. This list of supports goes on and on, but you get the idea. So, after you have fed them, they may leave and go on to the next watering hole or feeding spot. You will be left with a good feeling that you were good to someone and assisted them in a time of need. Others will feed and then hang around to receive more. All patience is paid off when you feel the need in you to give to another. This need is then given over to those parts of you who feed or nurture your own needs. As you begin to use this part of you that nurtures, it may be totally out of balance. It may siphon off more of you than is necessary and the person you are feeding will back off out of overindulgence, or he will move to get out of the way of the overflow.

You may find that as you begin to feed off of one another you also learn to depend on the ones who feed you. When that individual feels drained and says, "Enough is enough." You may feel hurt and angry that you may no longer feed at your convenience. You may find it hard to accept the fact that you now have to take responsibility for your own nurturing and your own energy. As you learn the difference between giving and taking you will come into balance and no longer give out of desperation, and you will begin to receive with love and not overeat or overstuff yourself.

All of nature feeds off of itself and you are no exception. You begin to balance when you begin to allow this flow with no interference and no limitation placed on either the nurturing soul or the receiving soul. You must learn to share. Sharing is not what you believe it is. It is the basis of all love and it is not taking what you want from anyone out of a need to fulfill yourself. You must take responsibility for your own rise up out of density. No one else can raise you up but you, and you cannot take away from another what you think you need to get you to your heaven on earth.

❧

As you begin to realize that all consciousness is shifting within your own beingness, you will find it quite easy to allow yourself the space to adjust. You will find that you no longer carry judgments against yourself for matters that you do not understand. Most of what you believe to be judge-able is actually the stuff you do not like. When you do not like a part of you or all of you, you begin to shut down that part or the whole, whichever the case may be.

As you learn to accept all parts of you, you will also learn to accept your ability to perform in areas where you thought you had no right to perform. This is true when you begin to know your soul. Your soul may tell you to be calm and allow all to pass while your nervous system is telling you that you must retaliate or take action. Your soul will advise you to stay calm as it knows that you are a peace loving entity. Your nervous system, however, will predetermine a situation and want you to take control, and be in charge, and get a grip on the situation to avoid future pain and future complications. Your nervous system is nervous. Your soul is calm.

Your soul says, "Stay calm, there is really nothing to fear." Your nervous system rings bells and sets off alarms and says, "This is not comfortable. This does not feel safe." He also says that you are not in your proper place and that you must move. He also says that you are not good enough to receive a good outcome to any given situation and, therefore, your situation is dangerous. You will find that as your soul begins to take over, he will calm you down. He will advise you to stay peaceful, and he will feed you light instead of fear.

You are learning to walk in balance and you are learning to walk in peace. Fear is a very strong magnet and it will be pulling at you from time to time. This is simply what magnets do. If you do not wish to get sucked into its magnetic field then you must rise above it. You are now making a pathway up and out of your current fear-filled life and you are rising up to a wonderful new light-filled life. As your life becomes totally light-filled, you will not panic as you will know that light is directing your life. The light is taking over and it is beginning to make you feel as though you are in a tug-of-war. This tug-of-war is the feeling that you experience when you judge yourself for not trusting a situation. Once you learn to trust, you will also trust yourself and all action or non-action that you take regarding any given situation.

These are great times of change and the revolution that is taking place is right inside of you. You are beginning to evolve and transfer energy into new areas of you. You are creating a brand new you who is going to be all that you like and, eventually, all that you love. You are the best of both worlds and you are also the best of you. You have much to offer to yourself, and when you begin to work with yourself and not against yourself, you will be allowed the peace you seek. Struggle only comes from fighting yourself and your choices. You are creating you and then you move in and complain about what you have created.

You will find that, as you move into your future, you will become more and more adapted to who you are.

You will come to realize that creation is simply a creation, and you are simply the soul of this creation. The creation does not matter in the least, as long as it has soul. You fill you up with soul and you have music. Music is a note, or series of notes connected together to create a melody. You may be confused and create a chaotic melody, or just plain noise, or you may get yourself together enough to create a beautiful symphony. You may be the judge of what you create and you may change it as often as you like. You are the writer, the conductor and the musician. You are also the audience. So, what is your pleasure? Does it give you pleasure to create a waltz out of your life or do you prefer a rap tune? It is all up to you and it is all simply a matter of choice.

You may even begin to create new types of music that have never before been heard. You may do it all or you may do simply one song and repeat it over and over again. A song is simply a melody with words, and words are simply a vibration, as is all sound. So, do you like the vibration you are creating or are you disapproving of your vibration? If so, simply change your tune until you find one you like. You are the creator of your world and you may conduct the symphony of your life in any way that you wish.

You are now moving into an area that will be most confusing to you without inner guidance. This area is upon you now and it is called today. You are moving into today and out of yesterday. Your next step will be tomorrow and then you will be out of touch with your past as you have known it. It is okay to leave your past behind and simply walk away. It is okay to leave the part of you that you are taking off, and it is okay to walk away and never look back. You are beginning to move into tomorrow and you will find that you will easily conform and flow with all that is waiting for you.

You will know that your tomorrow is part of you as well as your past was once part of you. You will know that you may leave at any time and not become part of any specific time. This is your intention. Your intention is to free you up so that you will no longer be part of who you believe yourself to be. You will simply be part of the whole, creating from the whole.

As you move deeper and deeper into your past, you are actually releasing yourself from it. It is a process of acknowledgment that allows you to let go and be free of it. This process also allows you to create a less confused and a less traumatic future for yourself. You will be allowed to follow a format that is most conducive to your spirit. You will begin to create from spirit without interference from fear or trepidation. You will learn that as you move within you and discover more about your programming, you will find that it is stuck to you like mud would stick to your skin. It is encrusted and you are cracking it off in chunks and washing it away.

As this programming gets washed away, there is a great deal of new input to balance the space where you have just cleared false beliefs. This space is now filled with new concepts and ideas and information that is being brought forward in your consciousness. This new information is often accepted and put to use as a stabilizer. Often this new information is accepted at face value and then it must "fit in" to the space available. This can cause certain problems to occur, as this space is often so "wired" from the previous tenant or information that this charge affects the new tenant or new information.

You will find that as you begin to refill future spaces that have been vacated, you will search for correct information that will give the best association between the body, the soul, and the wiring that connects them. This wiring is, of course, energized with yesterday, today, and tomorrow and it filters out what is necessary to create a new today, void of attachment to yesterday; to activate the new tomorrow that you are currently creating. You see, a new tomorrow is actually made up of past yesterdays and future todays that caused action and reaction to create life and living. Now all of these actions and reactions must be reassembled within the cellular system, in order to change them from the old future with the old past into the new future with the new past.

You see, if you can go back and look at your past through eyes of awareness less all the judgment, you can effectively change not only the present day created from that past, but also the future that will come from such a past. Not only do you *shift* today and tomorrow, you also *shift* the past and it becomes new and re-created. You can go back and do it again without dying and coming back to do it again. You do this through consciousness. This is your creative juice. Consciousness will set you free. You are becoming conscious now. This is also how you will rise to ascension. This ability is available to each and every one of you. You are just now beginning to see how much you know without knowing that you did. You are just now beginning to see how much you are without knowing that you were. You are here now and this is good!

∽✹∾

You will find that you are now turning into a very *sensitive* body. You are beginning to open up to your own signals and to receive incoming signals. This will allow you to know, in advance, how you feel concerning certain events and it will allow you to receive information from others concerning how they respond to certain events. For example: if you are in a train depot and you decide to take the "A" train, you might feel a sense of urgency that you should wait and take the "B" train. As you "feel" this sense of urgency, you wish to share it with your fellow passengers. You decide it would be best to warn everyone about your sense of uneasiness concerning train "A." The only problem is that when you warn the others, they begin to feel uneasy and think that you are spoiling their day by causing this uneasy feeling concerning the "A" train. You see, they want to get to their destination as quickly and conveniently as possible, and you are simply causing them to fear and make a simple train ride into a dangerous choice.

So, what do you do? I suggest you keep your own counsel. You are not here to wake up the rest of the world. You are not here to save the rest of the world. You are here to learn to use your own ability to see and feel and it is to be used for your growth and your development. As you turn away and go to wait for the "B" train you will feel sad and anxious for the others, but they stayed to ride the "A" train out of "free will choice." It is how you each learn and it is how you each develop into the soul that you are. You will find that your sensitivities will improve greatly as you go along your "path to higher consciousness." Do not blame the others for not feeling what you feel and do not force them to listen to your explanations of what you know. You are you living in you and they are themselves living in their own world and body.

No one owns another and no one must enforce his or her feelings, beliefs, or ideas on another. Offer if you are truly asked, but often they do not really want to know. Keep your own counsel and become all that you can be. Sharing is not saving the world and sharing is not telling everyone what they can or cannot do. You will learn to share without even giving a single penny or piece of property. You will learn to share of yourself by allowing others to be who they are and by allowing you to be who you are. When you try to force-share to get someone to see your point of view, you only create greater conflict. Allow yourself to know what you know without conflict. Allow yourself to catch the "B" train and do not listen when they tell you that you are being paranoid. Yes! You do overreact and yes, you do get paranoid, but listen to your own system of inner workings that will let you know how to get from point "A" to point "B."

You are learning to trust you and part of this is to trust your sensory input and output. You are cleaning up your act, and your sensory system is beginning to work for you. You will find that as you begin to be more and more sensitive, you will feel as though you are overreacting. You are learning to be all that you are, and part of all that you are is the sensitivity to know *in advance* that a situation is unsafe or uncomfortable for you. Get off the "A" train and take the "B" train, as the "A" train is going to break down and require a long repair on the tracks, with nothing for the passengers to do but wait in their seats for hours while the workmen repair the engine.

There! You just saved yourself several hours of inconvenience. This is how your sensitivities can work for you. No big deal really. Just a nice little system that helps guide you through your days and also helps create a flowing life. You are now on the "B" train headed home and you pass the "A" train and you think, "Oh good, I listened to myself and now I will be in time for dinner." This is how your psyche works. Every part of you is here to assist you, and it is now beginning to do its job. You are now allowing that "knowing" part of you to wake up and work for you

৯৬৶৶

You will find that as you begin to clear cellular programming, you will begin to feel at odds with your own self. You will have some confusion as you decide what choice to make in any given situation, and you will have confusion regarding your own feelings and where they are coming from. You are just now beginning to open yourself to receive new thought and let go of old stored negative thought. This thought, that has been stored in each cell of your body and neatly tucked away, has always been in the driver's seat and now it will rise to the surface and look for a new place to settle. This is judgment and shame.

Judgment and shame know no boundaries and spread over into all of your life. They are the part of you that is in your very physical makeup. They are the part of you that is in your very painful past. They are the part of you that does not wish to let go of life as negative. They want to continue to see how you will do under pressure from guilt. They want to see how you will live knowing that you are shameful. They want to be in control of your very existence and to be in control of your turning away from the light. You are not here to allow shame and guilt to bind you and to hold you down. You are only here to see how you will rise above all of this dictatorship that calls you bad, or evil, or nasty. You are not now, nor have you ever been, bad, or nasty, or evil. You are simply acting out an emotional trauma and acting out what you feel.

If someone gives you a hard time about what you feel, you must allow yourself to be right. Allow yourself to know without denial. Allow yourself to see without sharing what you see. As you begin to share all that you see, you are simply sharing your perspective. As you now know, the only way to share a perspective is through consent or agreement. One must know what it is to stand in your position and "feel" from your position. One then must agree on the outcome and move into agreement concerning what you are viewing. This is how you create hallucinations that are shared by many, and it is also how you create mass illusion which is what is available to you now under the title "creation."

As you move from one position into the next, you begin to see how you are not only viewing from a level of shame and guilt; you are also reacting from a level of shame and guilt. The greater the shame and guilt, the greater the conflict is within you. This creates a great dislike for anyone who opposes your view, as you will feel that this individual is actually loading more guilt and shame on you by not agreeing with you. If your investment in guilt is great, your opposition to any individual will also be great. This is actually the basis of much fighting and arguing. The point is made by the one who gets to air their point of view and be accepted by all as correct. The actual outcome is then agreed upon by those who discuss whatever topic was to be debated. As you come out of debate, you will find that you actually have no more of an investment in one way of seeing it than you do in the other.

You are here to learn. And one of the things that you are learning is how to be who you are. You are all parts of you and you express all parts of you. You are learning to not judge you as you rise to the surface. You are learning to allow you to express all parts of you and you are learning to not be afraid to be who you are. As you move into an area of acceptance, you will find it much safer to be you, as you will not be judging you so much. As you begin to release judgments against yourself, you will also begin to release your hold on guilt and shame. After all, how can anyone who is love be guilty and shameful? You are simply confused and it is time to rise up out of your confusion. You are not here to sit in the darkness of confusion; you are here to sit in the light of love and awareness.

Shame is the final hold over you. Shame was meant to keep you within certain boundaries and limitations and it is no longer necessary. No one need feel shame and no one need experience shame. Be free of shame by allowing all to be allowed to move within you and accept it for what it is – an outdated, no longer necessary, dense energy. Walk away from shame and know that you have no boundaries or limitations.

*A*s you begin to grow in awareness, you will begin to know that you are not all that you once believed. You will begin to see how you can create your reality by simply *knowing* your reality. As you begin to know more and more, you will find that you are more inclined to sit back and allow reality to unfold for you. You are very much a part of your current reality and you are very much a part of other realities that you are not even familiar with. You may be the apple of your mother's eye in her reality and you may be a hated boss in your subordinate's reality. You may wear the mask of the gentle lover and friend for your mate, and then put on the mask of teacher and disciplinarian for your children. You have many realities that you project into and out of.

You become a friend and are projected into your friend's reality by consent. You then decide not to play the friend role and your friend gets upset with you because he now has a missing place in his reality. He has a role that he wants filled and he had decided on you to fill that role. You, however, have decided that you do not wish to play his role that was written for you by him. You see, when you play in someone else's reality, you play by their rules for it is their reality.

One of the greatest problems we have at this time is ownership. You all think that you own one another and can tell one another how to *act*. This is due to the fact that you are getting carried away with your role as director. It was originally decided that you would put out a casting call and allow volunteer actors to show up and display their talents for you. You would then decide who you would cast in what role. The problem now is compounded, and instead of casting for a role you simply make up your mind to turn someone into this type or that type of a personality. You are foregoing the volunteer step and telling the doctor that he must play the plumber. You also tell the cowboy that he must play the lover and the newspaper boy that he must play the adult.

You are not allowing what is, to be what it is. You are so desperate for love and sex that you force love and sex on those who are not here to play that role. Then you cry and feel wounded when they run. They came into your life to play a different role, but, since you have no clarity, you get all the signals crossed and think they want something else. Now is a time for uncrossing your signals and getting clarity. Stop jumping on everything and giving it a role to play in your life. Some things don't even belong in your life, and often those things confuse you even more. There are many people and things that simply do not belong in your life. Of course, you are so busy hanging on to everyone and everything that you won't let go, so that everyone can move to their right place and play the role they are meant to play.

All parts are part of the whole, and all parts know exactly where they belong and how they fit in. Do not be upset when people leave you and move on. They are being guided, and it is really best for all concerned to allow moving and movement and change, even if you do not agree with the change.

❧

For now you are being as tolerant as you can of your shortcomings and in the future you will not recognize them as shortcomings at all. In the future you will recognize all parts of you as valuable. You will see how you are not in any way worthless, and you will begin to know how you may rise above all confusion regarding shame and guilt. You are not shameful nor are you guilty. You are simply walking a path for which you have no directions and no guidelines other than those left behind by earlier travelers. It's not so easy to follow a path without knowing where the pitfalls stand and how to not get sucked into the quicksand.

You are learning to walk your path no matter what and to know that the pitfalls will not direct your life, and it is not necessary to watch for harm as you will be warned in advance now that you are evolving out of the darkness and confusion. You need not fall into quicksand and if you do, you now know to stay calm. You have all had your slips and falls along the way, and you have all been down a road that caused you to return, or to simply stop and be aware of what was going on. Maybe the road was under construction or maybe the traffic was just too heavy for you to handle. It does not matter because all roads will eventually lead you home.

You are here to become light and to ask to receive light. You are here to become God in matter and the fastest way is to invite God in. Liane began to invite God in and she began to give herself totally to the idea that God could run her life for her. She had been so abused that she did not think much of herself and certainly did not value herself. All of that is changing now and I am teaching her that she does have value, and worth, and even God inside of her. She's not afraid of life as she once was and she is not afraid of God as she once was. She was often taught as a child how God would punish her, and since she was a child of sexual abuse she felt that great punishment would befall her. She thought that she was the only one who was having sex and being such an offensive child. No one else she knew talked about having sex or committing such grave offenses against God.

But then, no one else talked about much that they did wrong or bad. Only good things were talked about. It was a very confusing time for her and confusion creates great darkness, and the way out of confusion is long and dark also. Liane is not in darkness now. I gave her these books to show her the way out. She has done well along her return path and she is no longer in such great emotional and mental pain as she once was. She literally gave herself over to God and let God guide her. She let go of a great deal and changed her life dramatically and she is still changing and growing. She has created her own guidance by creating this series of books. This is no accident, she created this as a gift to herself and to show herself that she is deserving and she does have value.

You too create your reality and your life and your rise to ascension. You too create your own guidance and your own path to walk. So now you can decide how you want to create it and whether or not you choose God to be your director. You will find that God loves to direct and God loves to take care of his children. It is all part of this process. God will assist those who are willing to allow him in.

≈≋≈

As you begin to realize your full potential, you will begin to know that you are not only worthy you are the best. You will begin to see how not only do you shine like a bright star but you also carry the light of this universe deep within you. You may let that light begin to guide you. The light is God. You are God. This is God. You have tapped a source that is deep within you, and it is the life and the love of this galaxy and it can move you to write or it can move you to create miracles. Liane is not the only one to tap into her light source, you may also. You are all capable of such beauty and intelligence. It is all right here within you waiting to be discovered.

You are each here to perform a service and for some of you it is as simple as waking up. For others it is as simple as becoming aware that you are much greater than you once thought; and for still others it is as simple as tapping into a consciousness and intelligence that has always been a part of you, but you did not accept it or want to own it out of your own desire to punish you. You are coming out of punishment, and as you do you will begin to accept greater and greater levels of yourself as yourself.

So; who writes these books? It is God. It is Liane. It is the light that lives and is giving birth within her. It is that part of her that is alive with love and is alive with energy. She can tap into a mind that is the mind of God and no, it is not out there in the sky somewhere. I come from deep within the recesses of your own self. How can you not love the self when you each contain such glory within you? You are the glory. You are the wonder. You are the majesty that you so admire when you worship gods. You are "all that is" and yet you feel beneath God. You are not beneath God. You literally carry God around inside of you day after day. It is as though you are with child and you do not know that you are.

You are the glory and the wonder and yet you cannot get in touch with that part of you. You cannot hear the heartbeat of that unborn part of you. Oh, but you will. And it will come to you like thunder in your ears and it will wake you out a sound sleep as I have often waken Liane, and it will be the heartbeat of God and it will be the joyous rising up of humanity, and you shall be so grateful that you are who you are. You will rise up in awe and you will know that you are blessed and loved by God. You will no longer feel suppressed and put down. You will take your rightful place as the sons and daughters of creation and you will know that you are the light from which you sprang. You are the exact same light from which this information flows. You are the glory and the wonder of this entire creation, as you are the creator and you are the created.

You may see yourself as small and insignificant but you are not. You are vast and so very royal! You are the king of king's and you are the light of life! You are the joy and wonder of creation and you are the sweetness and love of God. You are special! You are mine and I am yours. I belong to all who care to seek me out and I lie right here inside of you. You are me. I am you and we can not be separated... not ever!

꧁꧂

When you begin to realize how all of creation is created by you, you will begin to take responsibility for your creation. So far you seem to blame God for the really big stuff and blame yourself for the day-to-day stuff. It is all you! If you have a miracle in your life, you created it. If you gave birth, you created it. If you've channeled thirteen books by God, you created it. You are the creator and you are creation watching the creator. You are both ends and everything in between. You are the cook and you are the stew. You created all by your attitude and your belief. If belief is strong enough and centered in desire and coming from love you may create anything you wish.

You are so bountiful and you do not realize your own resources. You are so valuable and you don't even know how to turn the knob that turns you on and makes you create miracles. You are stuck inside of a body and a psyche that you not only do not know much about, you do not care much about. You are in you and you are so panicked about your feelings and urges that you get all confused and misguide your own self. You have feelings and emotions and yet these are the very gifts that frighten and confuse you. You are afraid to be used and you are afraid to not be used. You are afraid to become known and you are afraid that no one will know you. You are afraid to hide yet you are afraid to come out of hiding.

Your feelings have ruled over and guided you for so long now that the *shift* to spirit may be a little troublesome for you. You are not accustomed to listening to spirit, you are more accustomed to following your fears. Your fears have lead you astray and now your spirit is leading you back to you. Your spirit is operating from love and not from common sense and logic. Do not expect common sense and logic to prevail. You are now moving into the uncommon and totally illogical realm and it is not run according to your plan. Illogic and unaccepted beliefs are often what keep you going. If you had nothing but logic you would curl up and wither away. You need dreams and high hopes to keep you creating. After all, how can you write books for God if you are coming from logic? And how can you communicate with God if you are being logical and showing common sense.

God does not belong on earth and this is well known and accepted. The common belief is that God resides in the sky or some far off place. The common belief is that God does not talk to anyone. You simply talk to God in prayer and that's enough. The common belief is that you visit God each weekend in church. But don't get too attached to God. I mean, he is in church and the church is the house of God, but that's just symbology to give you an idea of his presence. God would never be in you according to logic for that would mean that he is in everyone, even the guy who abuses his five year old daughter and even the guy who just shot the mailman because he didn't like the letter he delivered. If everyone were God, how could you all cope with that illogical fact? God is pure and God is clean. God does not dirty his hands with bloodshed. Well, there are those exceptions in the Bible were God did ask for bloodshed, but we can forgive him that and still worship this image. He must have had his reasons.

Your logic is totally illogical and it is ready to collapse. Your lives and excuses are no longer hiding the truth, and logic and common sense are flying right out the window with their inability to cope with true reality. The truth is moving forward on the wings of spirit and the truth is that you are all God and you are all capable of miracles. Once you learn how to create them you will be very happy to discover how you are God. Some of you may even create them and then live in the wonder of them before you see how you created such a beautiful gift. You are truly amazing in your ability to deny your own ability and your own creative power. You are also amazing in your ability to put yourself down and make others more important. Some of you actually put others down and make yourself more important, but you too will learn the value of each individual to the symmetry of the whole.

You are all coming into balance and coming together like a giant mound of clay that is shaping itself into life. You are beginning the process of elimination that will allow you to keep what works and to let-go-of what does not. You are moving into you and taking over you as never before. There will be nothing logical or common about any of these events. You are literally creating you and becoming you at the same moment. This is truly a miracle!

❧

You are not the being who once began this journey through space and time. You have accumulated parts and discarded parts until you are no longer recognizable. You have become opposite of what you once were and now you are returning to that you. This change that is taking place within your cellular structure is quite big and will most definitely be felt in many ways. This shift in perception and awareness may take several years and you may feel like you are falling apart at times. Of course, you are falling apart and losing parts of yourself, but, for the most part, these are unnecessary parts that once served to keep you down.

That was wonderful when what you wanted was to be down and anchored. Now, however, you wish to rise up and to do so you must lighten your load and you must shift to a new level of consciousness.

As you begin this shift into your new future, you will be reminded often of your old programming and your old value system. This is part of your struggle to rise freely. You are still attached in various ways to old beliefs and so you will see those attachments and be allowed to unattach and float free. Do not judge yourself for unattaching and being free. You are not alone; you only "feel" alone. As a matter of fact you are quite well received and you are quite well observed. You are very much in need of a good dose of humor in your loneliness. This is most important. Keep your sense of humor and know that you are loved and guided. You are so accustomed to living within the material world with all of its attachments that you feel lost if you are not attached. You feel alone if you are not attached and you feel left out. Be unattached for a while. It is okay and it is a good exercise for you.

As you learn to let go of more and more, you will begin to rise up to a level of perception that is quite relevant to your current situation. This level of perception is all that you can see from one position and yet it is unseeable from where you now stand. As you reach this level you will be reaching a goal that is like gold for your spirit. You will be reaching a level that will be so conducive to spirit that spirit will literally *glow* upon reaching this height.

You are now working for spirit, and spirit has certain requirements in order to heal and come back from darkness and confusion. Spirit requires love and light to remain. Spirit is love and light, but when the love and light were shut out of this dimension spirit began to fade. In the same way that a lighted candle will fade without oxygen, your spirit will fade without love. You are in a very weakened condition and spirit must be preserved and nurtured by feeding it love. It has been on a very lean diet since entering this dimension and now is the time to begin to nurture spirit. Spirit will grow big with nurturing and spirit will become strong and amazingly powerful.

You will find that as you begin to nurture you, you will be nurturing spirit, for you are spirit. You are body, mind and spirit. You are multidimensional and you are out of touch with you. So, as I guide you, I teach you to love each part and accept each part, and this will eventually affect the whole and everyone and everything will begin to "feel" this shift within the body of God. It is a soft and subtle shift right now, but it will not be so soft and settle in the future. It will begin slowly and then it will gain momentum and, as it does so, it will rise to higher and higher levels of perception, and these levels will shift into even higher planes of consciousness, until you are so insightful that you will finally know the truth of your own created awareness.

You are becoming much more than you have ever been and you are becoming much less in the process. This is evolution. This is transformation! You are literally becoming something else and yet not dying. It is sort of like becoming a cat when you were previously a dog, only now you still feel the urge to chase cats but you don't know why.

You are becoming all that you never were and you are letting go of all that you always were. You are becoming new and you are gaining insight into the possibilities of your creation. You are learning to rise above deception and deceit. You are learning to rise above all the unnecessary lies you placed around the truth to keep it hidden. The veil is lifting and the false identities are coming off. You will stand naked and honest and it will be very, very freeing. You will no longer feel the need to pretend and you will no longer feel the need to lie. It simply will no longer be an issue. Lying will not be necessary as all learn to accept the truth. You will not have to worry about hurting another's feelings because pain will become a thing of the past as you let go of your *need* for punishment.

You will rise to such levels that you will truly be convinced that it has always been this way, just as now you believe it has always been this way. It will be so much more of what you truly are and so much less of your false identity. It will be the culmination of eons of work and planning and it will be part of every one of you. If you are alive now, it is affecting you. Even if you are not alive, it is affecting you. You cannot 'not' feel it on some level. Even if it is only a spiritual shift you will sense this change.

Some of you will have, or experience, much larger shifts and they will be felt by you and for your own growth. This is all part of the plan. Each individual cell within the body of God has its part to play. Some are holding greater charges than others, and for them this shift will be quite profound and quite seriously felt within the physical, mental, emotional and spiritual bodies. This shift may be experienced as a mild headache by some or as a giant headache by others. Where you stand affects how you shift and how much awareness you wish to take on. If you choose to receive only small doses of consciousness you may only feel a little out of sorts. If you choose to receive large doses of consciousness you may feel completely out of sorts and a bit of a mess.

This messed up feeling will fade as you realize how you are growing and not dying. It will also help if you begin to accept all that you do as okay. When you drastically shift your consciousness, you begin to see things differently and yet you still have the old programming that tells you to chase cats. You will learn that as you evolve into your new identity, you will let go of all of your old ways. You will begin to settle into this new you and begin to look around and see what you can now do with this new position in creation. You will find that as you begin to become more and more of yourself, you will also become less and less of that other personality that you thought you were. You are now you and you also have many past you's, but you will find it most reasonable and most inspiring to stay this new you and not go gallivanting off looking for a new body to occupy.

You will find that you are the source, and if you are the source you will have no problem being whoever or whatever you want to be. The source is "all that is" and you may become "all that is."

❧

*Y*ou are moving into an aspect of your own self known as love. This aspect of you has always been part of you and yet it has never been seen. You have always thought that you knew love, but what you were sharing is not exactly the kind of love that nurtures the spirit and gives rise to your body. The kind of love I am talking about is true love of self. This love is virtually unknown by any of you. You are so accustomed to giving the self away to another in a gesture of love, that you do not realize that you do not know what you are giving way. Often you become upset when another rejects your offer and decides that they want nothing to do with you.

How can you love you and not know that you are too valuable to give away? How can you be so sure that you are not worthy, just because someone says, "No thank you, I do not like you nor do I want you for my friend." You are worthy, but why are you trying to give yourself away? Many of you are so attached to the *idea* of romance because part of romance is sharing in the partner's life. You often do not like your own life, and you wish to buy into someone else's life by selling yourself to them. Sometimes you literally give them a sales pitch regarding your wonderfulness. Other times you simply wait for them to come to you in need of friendship, or support, and then you begin to confide how you like this or that in a person, and so they begin to change into this or that in order to continue to *receive* the support you are giving.

Now you are both getting your needs met and it feels good for a certain length of time, and this is what you call love and marital bliss. This is not what I call love. Love is loving the self to the extent that you no longer need to fulfill yourself with another's support. You stand alone and you know who you are and you do not need love as you are vibrating love from your very essence. This is true love. This is not that warm fuzzy feeling of afterglow from sexual interchange. Love is much greater, and love will set you free of all the fear that has ever been. Love is so powerful that it dissolves fear, and it conquers nothing as it is not into being a hero nor a soldier. Love is brave in that it withstands all situations with knowingness and trust.

When you love yourself you automatically know that you are good. You automatically know that you are safe. You automatically know that you are you and to be you is best. You automatically know that you will keep you and never give up on you. If you had always known love you would never have created ceremonies to give away the bride. This is nonsense. It is not real, for you cannot give yourself away as the gift even if you want to. And who in their right mind would ever want to give themselves away for simply a ring and the promise of companionship? You are so afraid of being alone that you hook up with a mate, and you are so afraid your mates will not stay that you take out legal papers and offer a secure life to that mate in order to keep them. Why? Because you are afraid to be alone. You are not alone ever. You have a host of angels who visit and watch over you. You have other realities that are full of other you's, and you have this reality that is so painful to you that you want out of it.

You are not getting married out of love. You are getting married out of need-for-security. Your insecurity is great and it has been passed from generation to generation. Who created this ceremony called marriage? Your native forefathers of course. It was a way to gain more cattle for a tribe and more gold for the family. It was actually a tribal ceremony to give a dowry in order to entice a good match. It was a business deal and had little to nothing to do with love. It is still often a business deal and has to do with who has what and who can fulfill whose needs.

Your forefathers who lived in tribes were very superstitious and often invoked spirits to venture out and give them advice. This is how the original ceremony took place. A little superstition and a lot of voodoo type practices go a long way in creating tradition. You have ceremonies that you never question. You simply grow up and do what you are told and then the next generation follows suit. You are following one another into a blind tunnel. I am simply asking you to come out of this tunnel and *look at* what you are really doing.

You are now becoming what you have always wanted to be. You are becoming a free spirit. You are becoming free of restrictions that had been placed on you for eons. As you let go of these restrictions, you begin to see how you are not only being self exiled, you are also being self imposed. All beliefs have been accepted and locked in place to achieve a certain outcome. Sometimes the belief is so outdated that it no longer makes any sense at all. You will find that you may not be in charge of your beliefs at this point. It may be that they are in charge of you.

You have been rolling through life believing a certain way for so long that you no longer even know why you do so. You are so afraid to be you that you literally become whatever you are told is correct to become. If you don't conform to what is taught as normal, you become abnormal and chastised. So now we have you acting how you should and believing what you should, and along comes this series of books and you begin to wonder about what is really going on and how you got to be where you are in your current identity. You will notice that as you begin to *question* beliefs, certain individuals get very upset. This is due to the fact that what you are is what you believe, and in questioning belief you question the validity of the identity who carries this belief.

If you are coming from an evolved perspective, you will know how all beliefs are possible and acceptable, and you will not *hold* to any one belief above the others and so you will never feel the need to prove your point. You are beginning to see how proving your point is pointless and how you are never in just one point of view. You are in all points of view, as you are "all that is." You are the totality of created essence and you are literally everything at all times. You are the one who stands here or sits here and reads this information, and you are the one who does not accept this information and will have nothing to do with it. You are all parts of the whole and you only know how to use a pinpoint of your focus. I want to teach you how to use all of you, how to focus from a much higher perspective in order to see what is really going on.

You will find that as your focus begins to shift and you begin to see more and more of yourself and, in doing so, see more and more of reality, you will be surprised at how great and vast you truly are. Then you will begin to open some of your hidden talents and abilities. You will become more than wonderful and you will feel more than wonderful. You will feel that you are the one who created the world and you will be correct. You will not only feel on top of the world, you will feel that you are the world. You will feel that you are the one who is being created as well as the one who is creating. You will know what you know and it will not feel heavy. It will feel so good that you will keep it to yourself for it will be your special gift. You will have tapped your own resources and you will not wish to squander what you are.

As you reach this level, you will want to be free of all attachments to past fear and restrictions. Restriction and limitation have no place in the fourth and fifth dimension. You will be moving so quickly that fear must be left behind, as fear is a very dense energy and cannot vibrate fast enough to move into these new realms. Fear is being left behind out of necessity. It is too heavy to lift up, or rise, on its own. It must return back down to its proper place. Fear was never meant to rise. It was always meant to sink or bring down or go down. Fear is not to go ahead of you. You go ahead of fear. You are not meant to be in fear and to do so you must stay down. You are rising up and you will not wish to hold on to fear and stay down.

As you begin to let go of greater fears you will begin to rise at a more rapid speed. You will find that you are not only 'not' being held in place, you are finding a new freedom you never had. As you begin to move you begin to become aware that you do not know where you are going. You are in new territory and you are exploring higher consciousness which is a little different from what you are accustomed to. You are accustomed to being held down and, now that you are free-floating, you do not quite know how to handle it. You are suspended and not grounded and you do not feel comfortable.

This is your first clue that you are beginning to fly. You are not attached and you do not know how you got here or what is next. You simply "feel" like you have no direction and nothing to hold on to. You are in your first test flight, and you wish to stay calm and not grab on to the first piece of tumbleweed that rolls by. Stay in the air with no attachments and float. Enjoy the suspension and see where your life is taking you. You do not always need to be in charge by setting your course and planning your strategy.

You are learning to fly and you are learning to float free of this third dimensional reality. You are moving ahead and you must trust your inner guidance. Get out of your own way and allow something bigger than your brain to guide you. Allow spirit to guide you. Allow spirit to take over and allow spirit to be in charge. Step down off your throne of control. Step out into mid air and watch what you can do.

❧

When you have learned to unattach and be free you will find that you do not know what to do with yourself. You have been so anchored down for so long that you do not know how to fly. You do not know how to be free and this will cause you to become a little concerned. Know that you are being guided, and know that you are becoming spirit and spirit cannot be anchored. You cannot cause spirit to stay down as this is the time of spirit. This is the rise of spirit into matter. You are literally coming into yourself. You are returning from outside of you and moving inside to who you are. You are spirit and you are very, very powerful. This power is what will set you free. This power is not only you, it is your nature. You are literally a force of nature and you do not know that you are.

You are now in a place that we will call confusion, and this is due to the fact that you do not know how you are creating you and how you will end. This is not to say that you are not also confused by your own lack of intelligence. You not only do not know what is going on, you can't begin to figure it out and this gives you perplexity and confusion. You are now moving into a much greater area of understanding than you have ever known. This area, however, will be a little more difficult to handle because many of you do not wish to know the truth. You get frightened when you see what is going on and you don't wait to see the whole picture. You become upset and want to stop knowing or to change what you know. It can be as simple as learning that your child has been robbing houses and carrying a gun. You do not want to know this and will say you do not believe it until you see it with your own eyes.

You want to stay naïve for as long as possible because you judge carrying a gun and robbing. You believe it is bad so you cannot accept this behavior in your own child. You will learn that you are not bad just because you have a child who totes a gun. You are not part of your child in that way. You are not your child's identity and your child is not yours. You are you and your child is not really yours. So, once you learn to let go of the ownership thing, you will be able to see how this could be any child toting a fire arm. Now you are not so sure about what the truth is. Now you will use your intuition more because it is no longer *your* child it is simply a child. So now you wonder, "did this child rob at gunpoint or didn't he?" You are not certain and you don't really care unless you *know* the child.

Perhaps he goes to the same school as your child and even comes to play with your child. Now we are getting too close to home and must run and hide from the truth once again. This is because, if he plays with your child, then your child may have some of the same thoughts concerning owning a gun and robbing people. The key word here is "your." Once again, when we bring it back to *your* child, we have you in a tizzy.

So; I think that the most important thing to do for now is to remember that "God is in charge." Allow everything to occur without condemnation and allow everything to become what it is becoming. This includes the one that you call yours. You are moving into an area where you will no longer claim ownership over humans and this is why you see parents deserting children and children deserting parents. It is not wrong and it is not bad. You are growing and separating into all that you are, and this allows for all perspectives to be seen and acknowledged. You are not being punished, you are simply being allowed to see how you are growing and changing. Just because it does not look good now does not mean it is a loss. Everything is falling apart because it was never meant to stay together. Allow this separation to occur so that you can move on to the next step.

Yes! There is a next step, and the next and even more. There is so much more than you can ever know or handle at this moment in time. You are so very fragile that I can only give you what you can handle, and, for today, this is quite enough. You must have a certain amount of trust and faith in order to move into the future. If you have no faith you will be truly lost.

⚜

You are beginning to see how you are not all that you believe and you are not all that you thought. You are, however, much greater than you know. You are the beginning and the end and everything that goes in between. You are the last of your kind and you are the first of your kind. You will learn the most incredible information regarding how you are transmuting and growing from one thing into another. You are like a mammal who has decided within its own genetic makeup that it will grow wings and fly. Nature is changing and you are nature. Creation is growing and you are creation. You will see the most remarkable changes right within your own self. You will see the most basic steps of nature begin to reverse themselves and move into totally new areas of awareness.

You will see the most incredible transformation of any species to walk this planet. Are you paying attention or will you miss it? Are you in-tune or are you tuned out? You will find that you are no more important in all of this than a bug is important to humans. But you will also find that if you choose to take part and see it for what it is, you will become the focal point of all of creation. You will become the point at which creation shifts just by your acceptance and agreement to take the shift. You are beginning to learn that you are much more than simply energy that floats and does nothing. You are energy that creates and you are very busy creating you. You see, you decided to change the original plan and add a few advantages, so you are now deciding how you will go about this.

As you begin to shift your consciousness and add a few advantages into the scheme of things, you are triggering others to know that, they too, can add or subtract from the original creation. Messages are sent out from cell to cell within the body to communicate how you are developing and changing. Messages are also sent out from person to person to communicate how changes are occurring, and each individual decides to receive or reject such information. All news is passed through the entire body and, the greater the potential for acceptance within each individual cell, the greater the acceptance within the entire body or structure. If you are a cell in God's body, you are in a position to assist or decline to be involved. You are allowed to decide for yourself. If enough cells decide to change, the entire body will change and continue its path upward. If, however, the majority of cells are not in accordance, the body then remains where it is and does not rise up.

It will also be dependent upon such acceptance as to whether or not each individual rises. Now, however, we have a new twist. Each individual cell within the body may rise and reproduce and change and grow if it is so inclined, and it is self-sufficient and need not wait for the others for acceptance. Once this initial step is accomplished and the rise of the individual cell has occurred, it will automatically cause a magnetic pull toward the others who are undecided about their course of action or non-action. Now you have a series of events whereby nature creates its own special action motivator. It is a special need, built into each individual cell, to complete its cycle of evolution. This need is to rise up and to evolve toward the light and out of darkness.

So now we have our cells and they are moving and spinning and growing and accepting information that is being passed along the connective lines of communication, and the message comes to lift off. Some of your cells will hear it and some won't. Some will receive it and some won't. Some will know or understand the message and some won't. It will be disputed and neglected and ignored and transmuted and distorted and maybe even clarified.

Then, almost miraculously it will get through and be received for what it is. When this occurs, the shift within is commenced; it begins, it starts. Then there is the wait for more information and the opportunity for each cell to reject or accept it. Then information begins to flow freely after the blocks have been removed by the first pieces that were accepted. As more and more is accepted, the cell begins to let go of greater amounts of denseness and allow room for all this new "light" information that is entering.

So; as the dark information departs it is moved out of the cell and hopefully out of the body. How do you get heavy material out of your body? It is now waste product and must travel up out of your cellular tissue and structure, and into the elimination system. Then, if you are a student of these books, you are able to assist in the release of this dense, dark energy through a technique called enema. If you are not an advocate of this technique, then you may not be assisting your body in this area and it may become overloaded with escaping dense energy, and it may become toxic and harden in place before it is totally removed from the cellular walls. Now you have old dread, growing on top of new cellular information that wants to become your new joyous memory and tell you how wonderful life is and how you have risen to new heights.

As long as the old deposits remain in the body, they affect the new memory and they basically tell it to shut up and keep its place. Dark energy believes light energy to be dangerous to the body, because light energy will tell you that you can be anything and do anything. Dark energy believes this type of programming to be dangerous for you, and will keep it from you if possible. It is the same concept that is used by governments. Keep everyone under control by controlling the information. Now you know how you can grow out of the darkness that binds you up – literally binds you up.

You are free now to make your choice. Do you accept new information and give yourself the opportunity to rise, or do you reject wisdom out of fear one more time? It is okay if you do reject it because this information will continue to pass from cell to cell until you are ready to receive it. All information constantly moves in and out of the cellular unit until it is processed and received. This has been in effect since the beginning of creation. And each time the cell is able to accept more information, it is lifted up and held in place until the next step which will lift it a bit higher, until all steps are complete and this information has literally become you.

❧

You may begin to think that you are in an endless tunnel of darkness, but you are not. You are growing beyond your present limitations and this takes some stretching and searching. You are becoming "all that is," and this takes some great belief changes. As you change your beliefs, you will begin to change your entire genetic makeup. You change even handed-down patterns and you can change family patterns. It is no longer necessary to believe that you must carry on a tradition of disease just because it was originally activated by your parents or relatives. This type of behavior will cease to exist and you will become quite independent of such conditions.

You will begin to know that you are not only going to be free from disease, you will also know that you will be free from accidents. You will stop harming your body once you have let go of your need for punishment. You will also stop harming your emotional body. You will begin to heal and to know that you are healable and that illness does not have to lead to a permanent breakdown within you. You are at the base of these discoveries now and you are learning daily how to survive without harm to yourself.

This is all done through the transmission of information from cell to cell within the body. When enough of this information is accepted, it will become your reality. When you truly believe it, you will become it.

You are moving into a stage of development that is quite unique in that you have never crossed this threshold before. You have never before seen this truth. You have never before risen to this level of awareness. This is a first for you and, as with many firsts; you will find it a little difficult to adjust to. You are changing your cellular structure and it is bound to have an effect on you in some way. Many of you will feel great big changes, while others will simply discount these as the changes of aging. Both viewpoints are correct in that it is an effect of aging in reverse and it is an effect of rising to a new level of awareness or a consciousness shift. It is all the same and yet totally different, but it does not matter how you see it, for it is still what it is, not what you require it to be.

You will find that as you grow more and more aware of your current shift into awareness, you will begin to fill up yourself with this awareness. You will open to greater levels of information and you will allow greater levels to flow to you simply by this opening up of you. As you begin this ascent into greater heights, you will wish to know that you are gaining vast amounts of incredible wisdom and light.

You are accumulating light by allowing all information to flow and by not backing it up to stop its flow. You are allowing creation to flow through you and you are allowing you to become a conduit for creation. You are literally channeling creation and allowing or rejecting portions. You will come to a phase in your growth where you will no longer wish to reject any portion, and you will simply allow it to pass by without trying to stop it or change it. You will know when you have come to this phase as you will no longer feel the need to correct others or to leave them confused by your disagreeing with them. You will begin to know that you are part of everything and that does mean everything.

As you grow to new levels of agreement within creation, you will be growing to new levels of agreement with your own self, your own life force. This then puts you in agreement and out of struggle or disagreement or disharmony. Harmony will begin to arrive, and you will begin to know that all is well and all is moving as was originally planned. As you move into greater agreement you create a world that becomes agreeable, no more disputes, no more fights, no more proving you are wrong or right. It will all end in peace, and harmony will reign.

You are now at the turning point of creation. Creation is coming into its own and beginning to grow. It is moving and shifting and changing into its truest form. Do not try to stop or block creation by judging what you see. Know that everything has a purpose and everything is meant to flow toward the light. Nothing is meant to be blocked from receiving light. Light is drawing everything to it and, whether you like it or not, it will all be set free and it will all rise up; not just the parts that you like, but all parts.

You are not in your right place if you are fighting and struggling. Come to the light and know peace and harmony. Stop the struggle and let go of your hold on pain. You have lived a painful existence until now, but now is all that matters and now you are growing into your purest form. Let go of past hurts by allowing them to be seen, and let go of your pain by allowing it to transform into loving acceptance. This is not passive behavior. This is accepting that something much greater in intelligence is in control.

ﾉﾚ

You will begin to discover that you no longer feel it necessary to argue, or fight, or develop an attitude once you have learned to accept who you are. Arguing, fighting and showing an attitude allows you to rise to a position of authority and to feel like a know-it-all. Most of you don't really want to feel like a know-it-all; you just want to feel better about your hurt and low self image. You believe that if you can conquer and control, you will feel better and more on-top-of-things. But, for the most part, you only are left with a feeling of superiority and that quickly fades.

You fall into two categories. You like to fight or you hate to fight. You either enjoy doing battle or it totally drains you. You either enjoy proving yourself right and others wrong or it shames you. You see, when you prove how right you are at the expense of another, you begin to tear down the self-esteem of the one you are trying so hard to put in his or her place. The reason you are trying to tear down his/her regard of self is so you can have greater freedom or greater control. If you have given your power over to a certain individual and you do not like being in his or her control, you may begin to tear this person down in order to feel free of his/her control. In actuality, you are the one who has put this individual in a position of control over you by your compliance.

Now; here is where this gets a little tricky. Usually this person is providing your needs and in a position that could have a devastating effect on your position in life. This may be a boss or authority figure, or a friend who supports you, or simply a parent who is in charge of you literally. So, as you grow and change, you will find that you no longer wish to give your power over to another. At this time I wish you to remember that you need not go into full out rebellion as a small child might. You need only know your own position and suddenly begin to unbind yourself from this position that you originally created. It will be best for your own evolution to move with ease. No kicking and fighting are necessary. You needn't shock everyone by all of a sudden announcing that you are taking your power back and no one is ever going to control you again.

It is only necessary to become aware that you are in a position that no longer serves you. You need not begin to explain yourself to others because they probably will not understand it anyway. You need only stay calm and begin to realize how you are not in charge at this time, and how God will show you a peaceful calm solution to all of your big traumas and upsets. You are moving quickly now and you have not been in your right place for some time. You are now moving to your right place and it will not be a position of authority and you will not be in charge. You will, however, be your own creator and your own creative manifestation. You will also be your truest form and your most "light" self you have yet explored.

So, when the need arises to argue or to explain your point of view... let it go! Save your energy and save your voice and save yourself some confusion. If you can't say something nice keep your thoughts and your opinions to yourself! This saves you embarrassment and further self-incrimination. You all speak your mind and your mind is not yet hooked up to your spirit. Let your mind rest and close your mouth until you know what is going on.

❧

I will gladly begin to rise up and I will gladly begin to take over. I am not asking that you sit back and lose control and give in. I am asking that you stand up and give up and ask to be taken by Spirit. Do not worry that you will be harmed. You cannot possibly be harmed any more than you have already harmed yourself. Now is the time to heal yourself and to know that you are becoming spirit. How can you possibly not become spirit when spirit is what you came from and spirit is what you have always been? Let go of your belief that spirit is not you. Let go of your belief that you are not worthy. Let go of your belief that you are a sinner and begin to see yourself as part of a plan.

You came here to evolve and to rise up. You came here to look around and see what could be seen. Now it is time to leave. Now it is time to return via the consciousness. Now it is time for you to become all that you can and to leave behind all of your current programming and beliefs. Now is the time to become all that you are, and all that you are is truth, wisdom, light. You are an enlightened being. You are an enlightened energy force. You are a part of a much greater force and you are connected to "all that is." You are now channeling this information and you are now learning of your God connection. You will eventually learn that you are the center or focal point of your creation, and the way you connect with your inner dimensional self is to raise your level of vibration and give up your dense thoughts.

In this way you are creating a doorway into the inner being that allows you to follow certain neurological paths to reach the light that resides right inside of you. You are receiving and transmitting at all times and, through desire connected to love, you may reach right inside of your own self and bring all of this information forward or you may choose to allow it to remain dormant in you. Liane decided to bring it forward and now you see it in print. It is not so unusual, as it is inside of each and every cell. Want to reach it badly enough and it is yours. Want to change badly enough and it will assist. Want to rise up badly enough and off you go. It's no big secret and it's no big deal. It's in everyone, and everyone will learn to access it if they only learn to want it.

You are all rising and falling and rising and falling. The next step is to rise and stay, then to shift gears and rise a little more and stay. Then, once again, to shift up and rise up and stay, until you have reached lift-off and ascension. It will be glorious to see and glorious to experience. Right now you are in the beginning throws and you do not feel so good all of the time. You are stretching upward in areas that you didn't realize needed stretching. You are growing and learning as you grow. You might say that you are growing into you and then, as you accept what you have become, you will grow into more of you and look at that part and learn to accept that part, and then you will grow into even more of you.

You are becoming you by discovering you and accepting you. How can you know you if you do not show all of yourself to you? You must know who you are and what makes you who you are. You will discover that as you begin to discover all parts of you, you will begin to see how you treat others and how you treat your own self. You will begin to see your own programming by looking at others and how they respond to you. Do you turn people off? Do they want you to go away? Do you often feel like you want them to go away? Look at your feelings. You are wanting you to go away when you want others to go away. You don't like you and they represent you to you. You will find that you also may not like you if you always have to be surrounded by people. You are losing yourself in your work or in large circles of friends because you do not like you and you wish to lose you.

You are learning that not only do you not like you; you do not want you to be. You never seem to just allow yourself to be. You are constantly judging, and criticizing, and pushing at, and this creates hard feelings that create dissension, and anger, and frustration, and even a war or struggle within you. Leave yourself alone and stop beating yourself up for being human. You came here to bring God to humanity, so how can you possibly not be coming into humanity? Do not punish you for human traits or human programming. The programming is in place for a reason. Everything had a purpose and it simply got unadjusted or shifted into something other than what it was originally meant to be.

You are now in a position to look at a great deal of you, and, as you look at these big portions of you, I wish you to examine them and not tag them. No right or wrong tags please! Allow all parts of you to be. Allow yourself to unfold unto you without beating you up for what you are finally exposing to the light. You are wonder and you are magnificent and you carry the light of the world. Let you be as God allows you to be. Be patient with you as God is patient with you, and know that there is a plan and you are not simply a pawn in this plan, you *are* the plan.

You have begun to notice how God is part of you and how God moves you and even how God moves others. Now it is time to notice how you move God. You are created to be part of evolution and you are created to be part of the whole. The more you connect with God the greater your ability to reconnect all parts of yourself. As you begin this connection process, you will become familiar with more than one way to connect. There are many ways to be you and there are many ways to connect with all that you are. As you begin to learn how you have begun to rise to new levels of consciousness, you will be free to see how you are learning to connect to this consciousness and even to *direct* this consciousness into new areas of your life. The more complete this consciousness is, the more complete you will feel. It will be as though you are connecting, and growing from your own connection.

When you begin to learn how you are connected to everyone and everything, you will begin to see how you depend on others and they depend on you. When you remove the lines that connect to you and begin to withhold the energy you have been giving to them, they will *feel* this cut-off and they will feel they have been refused valuable energy. This is how you feed off of one another. Nature feeds on nature and you are just beginning to break this habit. Yes, this is a habit. It is programmed in you. You need not feed off of one another; you need only rely on your own source for nurturing. This is how you are learning to stand on your own at this time. This is why I tell you that you are being stripped naked to allow you to stand in your own glory. How can you ever know the glory and wonder of you if you must constantly run to another to get your needs met? You must now learn to stand alone and to know your own power, your own source, your own identity.

As you grow into this new you that is so full of individual glory and wonder that has been achieved by self evolution, you will find it quite easy to continue to live in glory and wonder. You will find it quite easy to live inside of you and you will find it quite easy to give all of your love to you and on to all of creation. Your love is your power source. You are turning into one of the most loving beings of your time. You are becoming a love machine that will continue to grow in love and to shine forth wisdom and to become the beacon of light that you were always meant to be. You are evolving into the best of you, and to do so you must release your hold on the fearful you. You will allow all parts of you to be seen and you will allow all parts of you to know that it was only judgment that blocked your evolution into forgiveness. It was only judgment that stopped everything and backed up the flow. It was only judgment that allowed you to become so dependent on fear. It was only judgment that showed you how unholy you were, and it was only judgment that kept you down.

You are now rising up and you are now becoming all that you once were afraid of. You will be free, and freedom frightens you and it gives you a way to avoid being all that you are. You will find that as you begin to become free, you will be faced with choices and decisions and you will be led into greater awareness regarding your own choices and how they might affect you. You are learning to achieve self-satisfaction in order to stop being dissatisfied with your own self. You are learning self-acceptance and this is very new to you. You will learn to be all that you can be, and you will learn to be all that you are by standing up for yourself instead of constantly allowing yourself to be judged by you.

You are the one who is killing you and shutting off your flow of life force. You are the one who is in judgment of your own evolutionary path. You are the one who will not accept you and open to your own glory and wonder, so now you are closed off and drawing from others because you have shut you down. You are not here to be punished. You are here to learn and to grow and to reconstruct a whole new you from the dust of what you once destroyed. This is the time for new growth and new insight. This new insight is based on security that comes from wisdom and not security that comes from a false source. You are your own source and this is what we are learning. You are your own source, and you are feeding you all that you need in order to raise you up to a level of consciousness that will allow you to be whole.

༄༅

I have been observing how you relate to all parts of yourself and to others. The truth is that you do not know how to relate and you do not know how to accept all of you. You have been so fragmented for so long that you are afraid to be whole. You are afraid to be alone or all-one. You are afraid to be all that you are and to know that you are greater than reality tells you. You are inside of you and this makes it difficult to look at all of you. You are connected to you and so you go into denial to protect your true identity from showing. Just as a mother cannot admit readily that her own child would rob and steal at gunpoint, but would readily believe that the child across town is doing such things, you are in denial of what is closest to you. You wish to keep it secret from you so that you do not have to correct this situation in you.

You will find that, as you begin to see how you function, you will have the opportunity to close your own judgment and self-hatred down. You will have an opportunity to become all that you are by accepting all that you are. You are all that you judge. You are human and you are nature and you are energy. Do not judge the very energy that makes you up and issues you forth. You are in you because you wish to learn to see everything within you. You have created form and projected into form in order to discover it more clearly. You are not only now the form you took; you are also the essence who entered upon completion of creation.

You will find that as you begin to rise up for ascension, you will begin to take form with you. You are turning on to the truth and the truth will set you free. You are growing in the body and causing the body to grow by doing so. You are rising up out of darkness and showing your body how to come alive to spirit. You are teaching you to become God. You are teaching you who you are, and you are teaching you to no longer fear and judge your own self and your own mode of operation. Forgiveness begins at home and you must forgive you for any transgression you may hold against yourself. This may be from the distant past or the current past or the present moment. You may even carry guilt from future projections, but for now we will deal with past and present.

As you learn to become all that you are, you will learn the importance of letting go of judgment against the self. As a child, it is difficult to tell you how good you are, because you are being trained to be "good" and anything other than good is portrayed as bad or wrong. It is not bad or wrong. It is simply that your caregivers and teachers did not want you to do what they considered bad or wrong, so now you have their belief of what is bad and what is good. I want you to erase it all. I want you to let it all be good and all of it simply a choice of what you want for yourself. This way you will not judge you for it. It is as simple as burning your fingers on hot flames. It burns! This does not make it bad this simply makes it a not very wise choice. I wish to get you to see everything as simply a choice. It is not evil, it is not bad, it is not a sin. You do not sin, you make choices and some are not very wise. That's about as evil as you get. You do not create evil nor do you become evil. You simply make choices that are not bright or enlightened.

Now you are learning to be smarter and you will find that, as you grow in intelligence, you will also grow in light. You will know who you are and how you got to be where you are. As you learn to be who you are, you will open to greater intelligence and greater insight into experience on this plane of consciousness. You are not all that you currently believe yourself to be, but you are all that you ever thought you could be.

❧

As you grow into your own beingness, you will develop within you the ability to be all that you are. You need not push or shove to become you. You need only love and accept you to become all that you are. Leave all else to God. God has a plan and the plan is in order. You are rising daily and you are stretching and letting go of the outdated beliefs and this will cause a certain distraction within you. You may find unease and discomfort or you may simply find that you constantly feel like you are losing control of your life. You are giving up control and turning into light. Light does not control, it simply reflects and moves. You are rising above control and learning to become a solitary support system for your own self. You are learning that you are your own source and that you are not all that you see.

You are in a situation that is most difficult in that you are not in charge and you cannot see (from where you now stand) where you are going. You are like a horse who is pulling a wagon and you are being guided by my reins. If you decide to no longer give your control over to God you may keep control and your old beliefs. No one is forced into recognition and no one is forced to let go of dysfunctional behavior. You may remain as limited as you are or you may go on and move into your future as an instrument of God. Those who decide to stay will simply wake later and be well received for their efforts. There is no race to become God and there is no time limit.

You will find that as you grow toward your unlimited beingness, you will begin to accept more and more of what you call love, as simply a way of being connected to those you wish to share your time with. You will actually rise above your current definitions of love, but, in order to communicate with those who are still in a state of semi-sleep, you may find it necessary to communicate from their level. This is not condescending and it is not lying about your own truth, it is simply a means of communication. When one speaks to a child who is new into this world, one does not talk above that child's head. You must learn to find common ground so you do not resent one another and create greater darkness and fear.

You are reaching a new level of consciousness and you will automatically draw to you what you need to continue your progress. Do not be upset if you do not communicate your progress well to others. Your progress is for you and it does not affect their lives in this moment.

You have an effect on the whole and that in turn will assist all others. You need not push and preach your truth. You need not do anything except love you and accept you. That is your one job. Love you and accept you! You are love and you are total acceptance. Become the love and the light of your world by allowing you to be what you are. Accept that you are love and you are light. Know it and you will be less hard on yourself. When you are less hard on yourself, you are less hard on others.

❧

As you move from fear to love and as you move from darkness to light, you will begin to develop a new sense of who you are and you will begin to see how you have been hiding. You are now being moved into the light in order to expose all parts of you. You have hidden certain aspects of yourself in order to protect yourself from you (the judge). You did not wish to be prosecuted and punished so you have pretended that certain parts of you do not exist. You have gone into denial and now it is time to come out of it. You are now going to admit to yourself that you manipulate and you control others, by certain aspects of your character, in order to get your needs met. Most often you are seeking power or to be on top. Most often you are trying to be "better than" or "smarter than" and you use this to show them how ignorant they are and this puts you on top and in the power position.

What I wish you to learn now is that you no longer need to control, nor do you need to manipulate to get your needs met. You are letting go of these false needs and, once you do, your need to be on top will fall to the bottom of your priority list. You will no longer feel the need to be right and you will no longer feel the need to be on top in the control for, or struggle for, power. Let go of this need and you will let go of a very big lie. Power does not come from a position of authority, power comes from within and power cannot be duplicated nor can it be acquired through control and manipulation. You must learn to turn on your power by keeping you calm and out of this power struggle game. You are not one unit trying to outdo another unit. You are not here to compete. You are here to find your place and walk your own path, regardless of what the current popular belief system may be.

You are not here to determine how another should or should not act or speak or live his or her life. You are here to create peace, love and joy. Do you have it in your personal reality or are you upset, annoyed, anxious and irritated most of the time? Are you stressed out and upset about your job, your neighbors or your school or government? If so – you do not have peace, love and joy. Stop teaching others how to think and how to see their world and begin to pay attention to your own. Teach your own self how to see the world through eyes of awareness and you will have a full-time job.

When you begin to see how you are wasting time and energy by teaching others, you will know that it is time to tend your own garden and raise your own level of vibration. You can do so much more good in this world by setting an example than you can by playing the "old wise one." You can achieve levels you never dreamed possible and open doors you never knew existed. I know that you are afraid of being alone, but it is time to let go. You may walk into a world of your own creating and, once you get there, you will find that others have preceded you and you are not so alone as you believe.

Please let go of this *need* to drag everyone up with you. You are not connected in that way and you need not cling to others for acceptance and support. Believe in your own self and trust in your own self. You do not need others to support you on your path. You need only walk your path and all that is required will flow to you. This is how creation works. You do not come into this dimension to simply buy your own home, settle back and die. There is more to evolution than achieving life goals and career goals. As a matter of fact, there is a great deal more.

This is all about being the best of you and knowing that you are acceptable and lovable. Once you see yourself as acceptable and lovable you will create a world of beauty and peace for you to walk in. You will see how you can and do create "all that is" and you will see how you are a walking, talking creation that was created by you. You are both creator and created. You are all that you do not accept as well as all that you do. You will soon come out of denial and you will know that you are "all that is" and you need not pretend that you are "less than" or "more than." You will simply *be*.

~ ❧ ~

*F*or the very first time you are rising above the material plane. This has been a plan for a very long time, but humanity has not been ready to rise above its anchor until now. You will see how humanity is in its right place and also how it intends to continue to evolve by watching your historical growth and development. You have not been historically evolved enough to do good as a way of life. You believed so strongly in good vs. bad that you often created good guys to make you feel that you too had a chance of becoming a good guy. Your only problem now is that you tear down your good guys at the first signs of human frailty. You are creating gods so you can destroy them. This is why you love your gossip and your exploitation magazines and tabloids. You love to see the gods fall because you feel that you are so much less than they are. You feel powerless to change and so you begin to destroy their character in order to make you feel better. After all, if they are not perfect in your eyes then they do not belong in a God position.

This is a time for letting go of judgment and for allowing *everyone* to be God. This is very difficult for you and it will show you how far you have yet to go to achieve awareness. As you begin to achieve some sort of clarity regarding this struggle of good vs. bad, you will begin to let go of the desire to preach any proverbs or to tell others how to live in order to achieve united awareness. Each individual has his or her own built-in guidance which will eventually lead them exactly where they are going. It is not necessary for you to teach and guide everyone else. I want you to focus on teaching and guiding yourself and I want you to know that your teacher and your guidance are within you. They do not sit outside of you, they reside inside.

As you begin to discover your truth, I wish you to know that it is your truth and it is not necessarily your neighbor's truth. You all get so sidetracked teaching what you have discovered, and yet what you have discovered is only a lost fragment and you try to make it into the whole truth. This creates greater distortion and also causes greater confusion and gets folks sidetracked. Allow everyone to walk his or her own path and do not feed them your truth, as your truth will lead you down your path and they too may jump onto your path and forget their own. You then have an overload on your path and this creates certain imbalances.

Bottom line is this: you do not do everything for everyone else, you do for yourself first. I know this is hard for you as you have been taught to straighten out others and to help fix the problems of the world. What I am now asking you to do is to stay in your own life and straighten out you and fix you. It is time to come home and stop trying to fix everyone and everything outside of you. It is time to use your energy on you. It is time to give to you. It is time to wake up and take care of your own needs. It is time to be who you are and walk your own path.

There are many ways to take care of your needs and walk your path without getting so involved with changing the lives of others. You may add to the life of another simply by supporting them in all that they do or by leaving them alone to do their own thing and live their own life. You have been so programmed to interfere and intervene that now you are terribly confused and stressed out because you take responsibility for others instead of allowing them to take responsibility for themselves. I will give you an example: You take your money out of savings to help a family member and now that family member is still doing what he or she has always done, and you think he or she should live differently and so you threaten to withdraw financial support out of the need to control this individual.

Live your own life; do not live in their life. The problem is not that you do not want to give more money to someone who is (in your eyes) irresponsible. The problem is that you want to control another's life with your money which was supposed to be a "gift" in the first place. If you want to give gifts or loans do not believe that you have any say over the results. Giving is letting go of. It is not having strings attached so that you may fix another or control another. This is a big problem you all have. Giving has nothing to do with ownership. If you consciously and agreeably buy and sell one another then you are still confused, as no one has the right to own anyone else.

When you have let go of your desire to tell everyone how to fix themselves, you will learn that it was always you who needed the fixing and then you will get to work in your own life. You are learning to love you and you cannot love you if you are constantly focused on everyone else and how they live. Live in your life and let that be enough. You are not so awful that you should not want to stay right inside of you and right on your own path. When you learn to accept you, you will begin to create wonder "in your life" and glory "in your life" and joy "in your life."

∽✿∾

You may remain as you are and never leave your current belief system if you wish. You, however, do not wish. This is why and how all are being moved at this time. It is not coincidence, it is timing. Timing is very important in the sequence of events that allow creation to expand and contract. It is most helpful to be aware so that you do not fight what is occurring. In fighting it you place great judgment against it and you drain you. Stop draining you, by flowing with life and by accepting life. Stop being afraid to be who you are and stop being afraid to see how you create all.

When you begin to see the dynamics that are part of each creation, you will see how you are each creation and you are part of "all that is." When you finally get this awareness, you will be more connected to the force that is your center and the source of all life on this plane. You are so confused by all past information that it takes awhile to get you unconfused and reconnected to the light. It is no longer necessary to stay dumb and blind, and now that the blindfold is coming off you may be offended by what you see. Do not be offended. Allow all that you see to be acceptable and know that you are being shown only what you are willing and ready to know. If you feel that you are too frightened to know your truth, then I suggest you allow yourself more time to be who you now are before you move into your new identity. You are much more comfortable pretending to be what you are not than you are being you. You will learn that it is okay to be you, and you will learn that all of those little thoughts in your head are part of your genetic and non-genetic makeup.

You receive what you wish to receive and you reject what you wish to reject. This is how you create and build you. You are no longer being built by you; you are now turning your construction over to God. In your determination to do God's will, you will lose some of what you consider to be important. You see, you work primarily from ego and God works primarily from love. You are controlling and manipulative because these are the survival skills you have been taught. God does not use control and God does not manipulate. God simply moves you in place to receive a jolt of new programming that will allow you to regain lost memory. Then God allows you to rest and restore before he moves you in place to receive another jolt for your memory. This is simply a process of allowing you to wake up without telling you what you are waking up to, or what will be brought to you next. This is why you must surrender completely to God. The greater the surrender the greater force with which you awaken.

So, basically, you are in charge. You may surrender and give up control of trying to do it your way or you may hold tight to the *belief* that only you know what is best for you. You have held to this belief since the beginning of time and I can tell you now that it is not working "for you." It is working "against you." Give up! It's not so bad. You don't always get your way once you do surrender, but look how ignorant you are concerning creation. If a child were in your care would you give in to that child's every whim, or would you curb his idea that candy is the best food in the whole world and television is all one ever needs in his life? No, I don't think you would.

I do not wish to punish you and take away your candy. I only want you to have the love you so desperately seek. This takes getting you off your habits and addictions. You are so addicted to what you think is good that you are no different than a nine year old who is left to raise himself and watches television continually as he munches candy and sips on soda. You are a child and you have locked your parent out of your life. I am here now and I want to show you the way, but you may not like all that I show you and you may resent how you must change and you may want me to go kill myself, but that does not change the fact that I am your parent and I love you.

You may shut me out or you may allow me in. It is your choice and it has always been. You decide how you will live and you decide who you let into your life. You create it all and you do not even recognize your own magnificence. You are truly out of touch with reality and you are in no position to judge anything as being good or bad. After all, you are simply a child and you think television and candy are all that matters. I want to get you to put down your desires so that we might show you your love. Your love is not your desire. Your love is not a need and your love is not an addiction. You are holding on to fake stuff. You must learn to let go of all that you believe fulfills you, because you are not being fulfilled you are simply drugging yourself further.

You will learn that you are not so smart as you think, and that in turn means that others who teach and preach may not be as smart as they appear to you. You, after all, are just an ignorant child who is still clutching to his candy while he screams at God for not letting him watch TV. You will find that you are not all that you appear and what appears to be good to you is not all that it appears. You have so far to go, and yet you have begun your first steps and you are in the beginning stages of ascension. Do not be afraid. Do not be angry. You only think you are losing, you are actually becoming "all that is."

❧

You will soon discover how you no longer believe in evil and this will lead you to goodness and love. It is as simple as letting go of a belief. Once you let go of your belief in evil, you will begin to see only good. You will see loss as good also. You will begin to see how losing can actually be a way of winning or gaining light. It is not always the winner who wins in the games that you now play. You will find that as you learn to play more and more appropriate games you will learn to be in your right place.

You need not play dangerous games and you need not put yourself in situations that cause you pain. Why do you think you risk so much? Why do you think you push your body to such extremes? Why do you think you hate who you are, to the extent that you are willing and eager to cut out the ugly and unattractive parts, and live with someone else's idea of how your nose should look or how your body should look? How did you get to this degree of self-hatred that you would so freely cut on yourselves and inject yourselves with all forms of chemicals? How did you learn to transform from ugly to beautiful and who told you it was ugly and who told you it was beautiful? Decide for yourself if you are created as you wish. Do not allow your fear of being accepted to drive you to change you. Once you learn how to love you, you will no longer see you as ugly. It does not matter how big your nose is, you will see the charm *in* you and you will love all parts of you.

You are not here to compete and win. You are here to accept all parts of you and to rise to your fullest potential. You get a little addicted and sidetracked when it comes to competition, be it sports, or racing, or beauty. You are out of control in the area of competition and I wish you to slow down and take a good look at how you are feeding your addictions, and feeding off of one another, and feeding your ego. This is a drug high. You get off on competition and you are using it as a drug. Those who win feel "high," those who lose feel "down." You get "pumped up" to play and you get overwhelmingly "high" when the stakes are big and you win.

This type of competition is creating energy imbalance and is causing grown men and women to commit all types of abuses to their own body in order to receive admiration and respect and attention. Receive your admiration and attention and respect from your own self. If you rely on others, you become their pawn. If they say you are great – you feel great! If they say you are awful – you feel awful, and you even try harder to convince everyone that you are not so awful as they say. You must learn to accept and love you no matter how others feel about you. As a matter of fact, you must learn to accept and love you no matter what you feel about you. In many cases you are your own worst enemy and you tear you down before anyone else can tell you how great you are.

You are killing yourselves with your lack of self love. You simply refuse to open up to you and to shed your own light on you. You have no problem adoring others and building them up. You do have a problem adoring you and building you up. Let the others provide their own light and you provide yours. This is how it is meant to be. You need not shine your light on everyone else in order to gain insight and love. It was taught "help others" because you do not know how to feel good on your own. Now it is time to "help you" and this will teach others in and of itself.

You need not preach, you need not teach from books. Show others by doing it for yourself. This will be communicated out into the collective consciousness and it will then become part of everyone and everything on this plane. Can you think of anything more powerful than this? Is this not how you will raise this entire planet up? Yes it is!

꧁꧂

You have all been in a dormant stage for many, many years. Now your dormant stage is ending and you are sprouting wings to fly. You are not so much beginning your life as you are beginning a new way of living, guided by intelligence. You are now coming out of the dark ages and into the light of intelligence and wisdom. You will seek information and digest it as never before. You will learn to be a free thinker and not conform to the old methods of mass consciousness. You are rebelling and breaking away from old limiting thought. You are allowing new thought to take you higher and you are allowing yourself to be your own power source. This, in itself, will create a wonderful shift in creation. Creation has always been so limited only because your thoughts have been so limited.

You will find that as you seek to acquire greater insight, you create a direct path into you. You are insight and you are wisdom, and each time that you strive to learn more regarding enlightenment you cannot help but go further into you; into your own beingness. As you enter you and explore you, you will find it quite easy to begin to know you. You will open parts of you that are prepared to give you all the information that is required to get you into the next level of you. You are entering you one cell at a time and exploring your own doubts and fears and, in doing so, you are releasing these fears.

Here is the catch: when you release a fear it comes to the surface and is *visible*. You get to see all that you are releasing. You are the projector, and you project this fear up and out and it reflects back at you. If you are releasing great fears of horror and chaos, you will see some horror and chaos around you. You cannot see what you do not carry. If you view horror and chaos, it is being projected from you. You may see it for a while and then rest. It may come forth all at once never to be seen again. Chances are, you will repeat it but with lesser and lesser effect. It will dwindle in size as the *charge* within your cells depletes itself. As you deplete these charged cells, you become less and less fearful. You no longer carry such great imbalance, and you are like a bomb that is being tampered with so that it has no charge left. You are slowly but surely being discharged. This is all done by way of you going within and caring enough to look at who you are and what makes you tick.

As you become accustomed to being discharged, you will find that the dramas that you once created in your world seem to die rather quickly. You will find that where you once held grudges, you will now let go very quickly, and where you once started arguments you now just don't feel like fighting back. You are being discharged! Your ego is sitting back, kicking off its shoes and saying, "I quit, I'm tired of all this nonsense." At this point you begin to know that you are in a winning position. Your lack of compliance to struggle or fight is your first clue. When you no longer care to prove your point and you move along knowing your own truth, without the need to convince anyone else in the whole world, you have begun to arrive.

I welcome you to the fourth dimension. The fourth dimension is a place of peace and understanding and it is one step closer to the fifth. The fifth dimension is where you strongly connect to your own God-self and you begin to fill with what I will call God awareness or the light. As you move into the fourth dimension, you will begin to feel yourself flow with all of life. You will move easily and follow where your life is leading you. You will not be afraid of your own choices, as you will allow yourself to take the position of trust that you have never before granted yourself. You are now becoming trust and faith. This is the place where it all starts and this is how you begin to love yourself as you did when you were angels. You will love this fourth dimension and it will give you the peace and calm that is required before moving on to the fifth.

You are now standing at the doorway and headed out of the three-dimensional world that you once required in order to hold your position. Now you are moving into a new position and I think you will like it very, very much.

❧

You are moving into a time that will be the most popular in your history. You will find that the turn of this century will mark a most productive age and will also mean the end of a whole way of viewing reality. This change will be drastic enough to be noted in your history books. You will find that as you turn this corner in history you will develop greater skills at insight and this will lead to greater awareness and love. You will be most often led to your own awareness and your own ability to develop and grow as an individual. This is due to the fact that you are breaking new ground and there aren't many who have gone before you in this particular area.

When you begin to realize just how great an event this is, you will begin to see how you are part of a vast happening. You are part of a great big birthing process and you are breaking free in order to become what you were always meant to be. You came here to participate and to raise this entire dimension into the next. You have come here to recollect this portion of reality (or non-reality) and to set it back in motion in a direction that will raise it back into itself.

You see, everything got pushed out and separated and now it is coming back in and together. As breathing in and out expands and contracts a body, so it does with creation. You are not about to end, you are about to become less dark and more light. Light weighs nothing.

155

Light is easily bent and moves. Light is bright and light creates growth. Without light there is stagnation and no growth. You are part of this evolution of creation and, therefore, you are part of light and dark. You are now leaving the dark and moving into the light.

Now; one problem will occur for many. You are not accustomed to the light and so it may feel uncomfortable at first. You may feel like you are doing what you do not really want to do and this will be your inability to be flexible and bend to the will of God. You are accustomed to free will and you are accustomed to screwing up your lives and your health and your relationships. When you must acquiesce to something that is not your will but God's will, you will find yourself wondering how you got in this position and watching to see how it will turnout. You will not feel exactly comfortable because only pain and confusion and stress and pressure seem to be comfortable and friendly to you. You are no longer accustomed to peace, harmony, joy and the flow of creation.

So, as you find yourself in certain situations and you are feeling bored, or feeling like not enough is going on, I wish you to remember your zing. I told you how you love to get all excited and revved up and feel your emotions fly. This is your addiction to zing. Now I wish you to calm down and learn to love peace with no emotional trauma or action.

As you move forward, you will wish to know that it is no longer necessary to create trauma in order to draw attention or to get what you want. You may walk through life very quietly and softly and never be noticed and yet be as big as God himself. How wonderful to know your own glory and to walk through the world without being attached to it. When you can achieve this state you will be learning how to flow with the glory and the power that is already inherent in you. You are the power. Hold on to it and stop zinging all over the place. Stop throwing your emotions around just to create a little excitement in your life. It takes all your time and all your energy to constantly fling yourself about. Stay home! Stay *in* you. Your emotional body is exhausted and overcharged. Begin to relax and don't get emotionally charged in any given situation. You are learning the way of peace, and peace will bring a great deal of joy to you on a daily basis. May you begin to walk in joy and see only peace.

❧

You will be your most powerful when you learn to allow all that occurs and no longer judge certain situations as not good for you. When you learn that you actually project all situations forth you will begin to see how you can let go of your dysfunction and your situation will change. Some situations will repeat themselves over and over again until you get real calm and stop kicking and screaming and stirring things up. You are not aware that you begin things by your accord. You are not aware that you push at others or simply imply certain conditions that make others think that you are volunteering to give to them. You do not get taken advantage of. You do volunteer without consciously knowing that you do. You all go back for more abuse in many different ways.

As you begin to see your patterns and to know how you are putting you "out there" to receive more, you will begin to consciously decide how you wish to behave, and you will consciously begin to know how you have always created certain patterns in your life. Look at your patterns. You all have them. You all create situations to draw energy "in" to you and, in doing so, you create a vacuum that sucks energy "out" of you. You are draining you by your need to drain another. You are creating struggle by wanting what you believe another can give you. You must learn to rely on you. You must begin to know that God loves you and God wants only what you really want, which is love for you and love for God.

You will find that you no longer have the need to get your "needs met by others" when you can lean on God and know that the universe provides all that is necessary. When you receive from God it is without strings attached. When you begin to receive and there are no strings you know that it is God sent. This is the true flow of creation and this is how all of creation was meant to be. When you begin to accept gifts that are universally given, you will feel a sense of overwhelming pleasure in that it will feel like something that you created and you received. It is! It is all yours and it was designed and created by you and it was returned to you. When you reach out into creation and you are pulling strings to get what you want, you are going to get your strings pulled right back. When you ask and creation offers to comply, you are creating giving and receiving. Be careful how you manipulate those around you, as manipulation only creates more manipulation.

Allow everything to be open and free to flow. No manipulation please. You are tying yourself up in knots by trying to manipulate others and by being dishonest about your intention. You are putting out to get back, and what you want to learn is how to give (no strings attached) and how to receive (no strings attached). This will be a very big lesson for you, as you have all been taught that you must return tit-for-tat, and that you don't just get something for nothing. You must learn that you have been incorrectly programmed and this will allow you to find out how you are programmed and to change it for a better way.

You are now at a very powerful turn in your road to created godliness. You may begin to regain power or you may begin to push out to get more of what you want. Watch your motives. Would you still take action if nothing was at stake? If you had nothing to gain or nothing to lose would you still create this same situation? You are not creating situations out of love of self, so how can you possibly say that you are creating out of love for others? You do not know how to love others if you do not love yourself.

You are now beginning to see how you do not know what you are doing and how you do not know what you really think. Everything that you do has an influence on what you create. You are now in a position to create love and joy and peace of mind. You are now in a position to become light and to let go of your darkness. You no longer wish to own darkness as you wish to rise up. When you begin to see how you are using your darkness to stay down you will wish to clear all forms of darkness in order to be light. As you move through this age of awakening you will discover that you are not alone and you are not a victim in any sense of the word. You are simply being you and you are simply being love. The only problem has come in the form of confusion that seems to surround you and tell you that you are not love.

As you awaken into the higher realms of your own awareness, you begin to see things about yourself that you did not know you owned. You are now in a giving up phase and as you give up or surrender your more confusing habits, you will become more confused. Old habits die hard and they do not disappear overnight. You are learning to deal with these habits and patterns as you bring them to the surface. You may find yourself wanting to give in to your old habits and you may find yourself wanting to repeat them again and again. This could be anything from the habit of chewing your fingernails to the habit of starting fights. You could have a pattern in you that desires chaos or you could carry a charge that is in need of punishment. When things get slow you may start a fight to liven things up or you may simply worry yourself into a fit of exhaustion. Over what? Well, when you get bored you begin to create all kinds of situations or dramas to fill the quiet space. You don't seem to do so well with quiet. You feel dead and not alive unless you are zinging and so you create all kinds of things to make you feel alive.

Now you are beginning to change and no longer want conflict and excitement in your life. The call for peace and quiet is quite strong, and you will be happy to know that you are actually going home this time. You are actually going to make it through this and return to peace. You are actually going to see boredom as a gift and no longer feel the need to get your body all excited through the emotions in order to feel alive.

You are going to put down your emotional dramas and begin to relax into peace and contentment. This does not mean that you walk around all day like a zombie with a smile. It does not mean that the conflict of your daily life will simply no longer exist. When conflict goes it takes stress with it. "No pain no gain" will no longer be true. You will gain and feel good with minimum to no pain. You will let go of the idea that you must keep everyone (including yourself) on their toes. It won't be necessary to push at others because you will no longer want or need anything from them. You will know that your supply of love and energy is limitless and that it comes from God and not from outside.

You will learn to love you as you have never thought possible. You will also learn to trust you as you have never thought possible. This is the time of grand awakening and celebrating light. You are moving into an area that is new to you and it is called *peace*. Are you ready for it? Can you handle it? Here it comes....

⚘

You are now in a position to be totally honest and know who you are. Being totally honest does not mean that you share your point of view with everyone. It does, however, mean that you are being honest about how you feel to the best of your ability. This still does not have to do with others. You need not give your power over to others by wanting them to accept you or by giving them all that they may want from you. When you are made to feel inferior it is simply your own mistrust coming up to say "you do not deserve to be treated well." You do deserve to be treated well and it is not necessary to be bullied by your own emotional insecurity. You see, no one can bully you, you must first be bully enough to put yourself down and assume the worst about you. When you assume the worst, you allow for hatred and anger to fill you up. This is due to the fact that you are light and do not wish to be put down, not even by your own self.

So, when you emotionally push you around and shut off parts of you, you begin to change what was created out of love into something else. The most important thing to remember here is to be gentle with your own self. You will find that you no longer need to create stressful situations once you begin to allow yourself to be trust. With trust you will learn that you are moving up and out of anger and hatred of the self, and this will be projected out and you will see it as coming back at you. You are not so much in a state of projected anger as you are in a state of projected fear. Fear is your biggest friend and it is the one who usually does most of the pushing and shoving within you. Once you let go of fear you have nothing left to lose. Fear is your last friend that you are clinging tightly to. Fear is your last relationship that is not working on a spiritual level. When you let go of fear you will be "free." No more hatred. No more anger. No more self-destruction.

You are going to have a little unease as you finally break up with fear. After all, you have been lovers for a very long time and you think you need fear to keep you safe. After all, fear is the one who has always told you to push back if someone is pushing at you. And fear is the one who has always told you how right you are to make others wrong. Fear has also been the one to tell you to run when things get too hot to handle. It is not that fear is bad it is simply not necessary any longer. Why? Because the light is here now and you will be directed and guided by it, and fear is no longer employed nor is it needed. It is simply outdated and moving into history. Fear is out, love is in. You are no longer fearful, you are love filled. With the light, come the answers and the awareness that is required to rise above any given situation. You may even begin to hear words of incredible wisdom come forth and you will wonder, "How did I know this or how did I learn this." It is the light speaking for you and you will feel it as you, as you are the light.

You must learn to lean on God and you must learn to know that God is in charge and God is in the driver's seat. You are becoming aware of God at the same instant that you are transforming into light. That is due to the fact that God is light and you are God. You and God are simultaneously being born, as you and God are one in the same. You are not one, you are all. You are not separate from, you are connected to. You are part of everything that is creation and you are part of "all that is." How can you possibly need fear when you are "all that is?" If you fear, you fear only you. You are what you are so afraid of.

There is a good deal of information that has not been delivered to you and it will continue to arrive. It is not so understated as this series and it will serve to assist you in your lift off (or lift up) process. You are beginning to see how you are not as smart as you once were and in the future you will become even smarter than you think you are now. You are beginning a path that will be known as ascension. You are beginning to rise above the dull existence of everyday drudgery and to know that you are indeed blessed. You are blessed with an ability to create all that you wish for yourself.

Your biggest problem in the past has been your desire to create a safe place for yourself which inevitably creates the belief that you are no longer safe. So, as you create from a belief that you are safe and everything is in order, what do you suppose you will create? Right. You will be put in a place where you create peace and harmony, or order. There is no chaos, there is only a belief in unordered events which gives you the idea that chaos is occurring.

You are moving into an area within you that will assist you in your rise above all illusion. This area in you is your center. You do have a center and you do generate "light" from within. There is nothing out there it is all within. If your light has been snuffed out or buried, you will find it necessary to ignite in order to rise up. In some instances this re-ignition process will be simple and in others it may take some work. It all depends on the extent of harm you have allowed within you or the degree of lack of self appreciation. If it is very low you may expect to feel very wrung-out at times. You may also feel a little more berserk than you care for. These are just symptoms and they are to be expected.

Sometimes you will clear huge doses of fear and you will feel very light and happy for days after. This is due to returning to your natural state which is peace, love, joy. You will, of course, have the opportunity to clear all fear until you reach a level that is conducive to the spirit. Often you will be allowed to clear your own fear until your spirit can grow strong enough in you to begin to dissolve fear for you. At that moment you will begin to make huge leaps in your advancement to the fourth dimension and on upward.

You are now at a place that is most uncommon for you. You are part God and part man and you are evolving, but you don't know exactly what the plan is. This is the plan: it is to arrive at heaven's door and to live in peace. It does not matter what you do, or how you live, or where you live, or what job you have, or even if you do not work. It has nothing to do with anything human. You do not plan as God plans. God cares little about the illusion you have created and are so stuck to. It is your desire to get unstuck and so we have begun. You see, you created a big rock and then you went to live on it and now you think that you and the rock are all that exists. It is just a rock and you are just growing on it like moss or amoeba. You are not part of this rock, you only think you are. Give it up. Let go of your rock. Come back and see it for what it is. You are being silly and frightened and clinging to it for dear life.

As you begin to evolve, you will see that *God's house has many mansions and they are vast indeed. You may choose to be on many levels at once or you may choose to be a tiny pinpoint on a tiny fleck in a tiny space. You do not wish to remain tiny and limited. You are ready to refocus and see the whole picture. There is so much more to see and there is so much more to know.

*Note: I thought this made no sense until I found – John 14:2 KJV "In my father's house are many mansions"

❧❧❧

*W*hen you begin to realize how you are not only the creator, but also the creation, you will see how you are creating all that occurs in your life. When you become calm and slowly breathe in life you exhale a calm reflection. When you begin to know that all is occurring according to your will, you will begin to realize that it is only you who needs to become peace in order to have peace. As you become peace you will be seeing the most remarkable changes in those around you. This will be your new reflection. Begin with you and you will be creating everything you see. How can that be such a bad idea?

When you learn to project this peace that you are creating, you will find that it cannot be disrupted by outside influences. You will stay calm and know that all is taking place as planned. All that is important is that you breathe peace. You will walk into a state of peace by first seeing peace. If you cannot see divine order, you will not create divine order for yourself. This, of course, will affect not only you but it will affect all that you view. You cannot affect others unless they are in agreement to see peace for themselves. This does, however, add to the community consciousness and to the overall awareness served by information believed.

When you walk in peace you allow the possibility for others to walk in peace. Just as a weight lifter might break a record for the first time after hearing how someone else had lifted an incredible amount of weight. He now decides to *believe* that he too can break the rules that keep humanity believing that "this can't be done." Once he breaks this weight record he will open a door of possibility to lift even greater weight, and then later on someone may come along and outdo all the records. This is the type of situation that is created by simple "awareness" that it has already been done.

As you begin your ascension process, I want you to remember that you are creating your own rise up out of consciousness by your willingness to believe in peace. You will find that not only do you begin to rise up, you also begin to open new doorways to peace and this will be felt by others. So, you do not create peace for others but you do show them by simply living your own peace. Boredom is about to become outdated as you begin to know that there is divine order even when you don't see anything being created. Learn to love boredom and to see the gift in not always being in the action. You thrive on action and excitement and it's time to thrive on peace.

You will find that as you begin to create new realities for yourself you will not always be ready for them. You may begin to create peaceful situations and then, when they arrive, you feel uncomfortable in the calm and start to stir things up so you can get your excitement going. Your biggest trigger for excitement in your body is fear, and so you learn to trigger fear so you can feel "alive." You are learning that balance will always come with time and healing. This is true with all life. Balance will come with time and healing. You are beginning to open and heal, and balance is your next step.

You are not a race of ignorant baboons and you do have mental faculties that will learn to assess your intent. Once you begin to understand your own workings, and how you create your reality, you can learn to project only what you wish to live with. You may project acceptance and love in all situations and what you will receive back is acceptance and love. Learn to overcome illness and pain by projecting wellness and balance out, so you receive wellness and balance back.

You will find that it is never necessary to "fight" with anyone or anything that is occurring in your life. Peace is peace and fighting is war. When you learn to allow action to take place around you and you simply pass through it you will be adding to your own *well*-being. Do not get involved in everyone else's drama. Be in your reality and know peace. Stop acting out pain and begin to act out love. You are now at a turning point in your evolution and the future that awaits you is quite beautiful and heavenly. You are walking to the gates of heaven and you will really, really enjoy heaven.

⚜

As you begin to grow into your new identity, you will begin to see how you are having some difficulty shifting up into higher consciousness. You are not only 'not' prepared to deal with everything from this new level, you are also afraid to be this new you. You see, you were always taught that you must act and react a certain way and the more you let yourself be, the more frightened you may become. Being is allowing freedom and you are afraid of the consequences of freedom. You will find that as you begin to be free you will begin to know your true identity and you will truly express love.

Here is how you learn to express love: stop pushing at you to do what you do not wish to do. Allow yourself to be free of limitation by allowing yourself to be unlimited in your choices. You are now moving into an area that is very new to you and you must be very patient. You must learn that God is with you and you must learn that you may make whatever choices you like. The free will choice is always yours. You are the only one who limits your choice by saying, "No, I can't" or "Yes, I can."

You will find that the more you learn about you and how you operate, the more you will begin to discover how you limit your world and how you could be creating from unlimited spirit. You are the creator and you are creating limitation out of the fear that tells you how bad you are or how wrong you are. Break your limitations and go into unlimited reality. You will find that, as you go along, you will no longer be pleasing everyone else and you will be pleasing your own self. Learning to please yourself is very good and will make you like you. Pleasing everyone else is very good and will make everyone else like you. You are here to learn to like you, and you are here to learn to love you. So, if you constantly try to please others you will be constantly pushing at you to do what they want you to do and to be what they want you to be.

You have come a long way and you will learn that the only one who will ever love you is you. You do not learn to love you by making you the bottom rung on the ladder. You must learn to love you by allowing you to be top dog and number one on your list of priorities. You are not in this to be left out. You are not in this to be made unimportant while everyone else in your life gets top billing. You are in this to be the best – to win your own love and affection. You will find that the more you can do for you the greater the chances that you will begin to like you again. It is simply a matter of asking yourself to provide for yourself. Do you provide all the nurturing you need and do you supply all the love and attention you need? If you do, you are centered and your love of self is intact.

You are now in a process of self-discovery and it is put in place by your need to be whole and complete. You shut down part of you and now you are about to rediscover you and to know how you are truly a free being with no limitations. You are being led directly into yourself and you are being prepared for your own arrival. As you travel into you, you will be interested to know how you got stuck in certain areas. You are moving and you are learning to let go of all your weight in order to move more freely. You cannot know where your weight is if you do not "feel" it and/or see it. This is why you now find yourself in situations that will allow you to "feel" the weight of the darkness that you carry.

You are beginning to move in a new direction and this will be out of darkness and out of pain. You are also going to play out your dramas in a more constructive way. You are going to learn that, you are not only being put in situations to assist, you are also being put in situations that you asked for and you wanted in order to trigger pain and/or joy so you could "feel" what you carry. You will find that what you carry is what you are made of and as you create a new you, you literally let go of parts and allow new parts to come forward.

You will be well-balanced and in good shape for ascension. You will have let go of guilt and judgment and you will have let go of pain and struggle. You are doing well and your efforts to let go are well worth your joy and acceptance. You see, you receive like for like. You let go of a big one and you receive a big one. One of these days you will begin to understand energy and how you live and how you die. For now, it is enough that you want to know more about who you are.

❧

You are indeed the one who is responsible for you. You are the one who changes you and you are the one who stays with what you desire. You are not, however, conscious of all parts of you, so you end up with a big tug-of-war. One part is moving in one direction and another part is headed in the opposite direction, and yet other parts are undecided. There are even parts that are running around in circles because they are not sure what choice is best. Let it all go! Know that God is in charge and God will serve each part in due time. You need not make yourself crazy trying to figure out how to be or who to be. Simply be. Stop pushing at you to be anything more than what you are. You are where you are for a reason. How do you know that you are not doing a wonderful thing just by allowing you to be where you are?

You are in a process of opening up and developing beyond your wildest dreams. If you cannot let yourself be, you cannot accept yourself and look at yourself. You are too action oriented. You do not know how to sit and wait for creation to be delivered to you. You are so impatient that you push out into creation for what you want.

All is delivered in good time. The universe provides for you and you provide for you from inside. You do not need to rush around like a crazed person trying to get a drug fix. You are creating greater confusion and chaos by doing so. You are also creating greater pressure on you to perform, which is not how creation works. You are not meant to be performers who must show up and act a certain way each day. You are meant to *flow* with creation and you are meant to be in sync with all of life. You got out of sync by not listening to your own inner workings. Now is a time for reconnecting and knowing that the plan is in place and you made the plan, you simply forgot that you did. Trust you. Would you create a plan that was meant to harm you or would you create a plan that would raise you up and elevate you?

You have come to a place that will begin to seem nonexistent or not really what you want. This is due to the fact that you are holding on to your old ways and old habits, so you do not wish to become your new personality because you do not yet trust this new you that you are creating. You are moving into uncharted territory and you are learning to become what you are moving into. Once you have established a base, you will begin to lock in and even grow roots in this new position. Then you will be uprooted once again and moved to your next level of awareness. The deeper your roots have grown, the more difficult it will be to pull you up out of each layer of consciousness. It is best not to *form* opinions and become opinionated. Opinions only hold you down and you will have a much harder time moving on and up.

As you begin your rise in consciousness you will take all parts of you with you, and you will see how some of your old opinions and judgments begin to fade as you adopt a new perspective from your new, higher position in consciousness. This is the *shift* up. This is transformation taking place within you. This is you becoming all that you can be by letting go of all that you once believed to be true. You are letting go of your truth to accept a new greater truth, and soon you will let go of this new greater truth to accept an even greater version, until you finally reach the top and see how there is no truth only truths. Everything is the truth depending upon how you view it.

You are the one who must live in you. You are the one who must be who you are. If you do not like how you treat you then I suggest that you change. If you do not like being sick then you may change your cause of disease by changing how you view all life. You need not rush out and do this or that to change. All that is necessary for change to take place is for you to *shift* your perception. You are in a state of constant turmoil when you do not trust you. I want you to be in a state of constant peace. Peace comes when you begin to trust you, when you begin to trust that you are creator and creation. You are in a phase of basic repair in order to lift you up out of despair. You are being fine tuned so that you might see hope and rise above all that you have created.

You will find that you do not always know how to fix you, so it is best to allow yourself to gradually shift as you would gently shift your car. If you push you too soon you will create some major damage and it will require more repair. You are not in a position to see where you are going so it is best to let God drive and let God shift for you. You are learning to be who you are and since you do not know who you are, you judge every little thing that you do as either good or bad. The things that you do are not good or bad, they are simply the things that you do.

When you begin to see the overall picture, you will realize how you are not only 'not' being so smart at times; you are also not being so dumb at times. The problem is that you may do or say something that is very smart and you end up feeling dumb and reprimanding yourself. You also get hooked on being right and then you beat yourself up for showing off. You are so mixed up and off-center, that it is best to not say anything until you learn to accept you. You will learn to accept you and you will learn to be all that you can be.

For now, to ensure peace, it is best to keep your mouth shut. It would be so nice to see you all being quiet for a change. So, for your own sake, begin to keep silent and breathe peace. Allow your quiet time to be a time to listen. Listen to nature and listen to what is going on around you. Do not add to the chaos. Be silent and listen. Do not stir the feelings of others. You love to impress yourself and others with your wisdom, and I am here to tell you that you have the story upside down and backwards. When you try to tell another how to live their life it is from your position. You do not know where they are or where they are going. It is their life and their path. Shut up and allow them to be them and stop trying to make them live by your rules. Your rules are as out of balance as you are. Do you really want to give advice and create another you? I do not think so.

When you begin to accept you, you will have no problem accepting them. They are very much like you in that they are God too. They live in turmoil too. I do not wish you to hand out free advice until you know what you are talking about. This could take you a very long time, so I suggest you learn how to stay silent until you can learn to carry on a conversation without trying to change the person you are speaking to.

This is good for now. Your assignment today is to go out into the world and listen, really listen. Do not judge what you are listening to. Simply accept and know that it is all true and it is all part of God.

❧

You will become so strong in your belief of ascension that you will literally rise above your current level of thinking and seeing. You will begin to see the most wonderful changes in how you treat yourself and, subsequently, how you treat others. You are most remarkable in that you no longer wish to be who you once were and yet parts of you will not let go of who you once were. You are beginning to become all that you can be and you are beginning to show signs of change. You actually see this change as vibration and you are being vibrated at a much quicker rate. This, in itself, offers you the opportunity to see things differently. With a quickened vibration you will receive more quickly and you will lose old parts of you more quickly. This has two parts and will be seen (by you) as good and bad. Lessons will arrive quicker and lessons will be learned and grades passed quicker. Not only will you be receiving answers quicker, you will also draw your next question sooner.

As you begin to arrive at this state of speeded up vibration I wish you to remember that you are releasing, you are not taking on. You are letting go of your old way of thinking and this allows you to take on a new way. It also allows you to see the old as it leaves so you can know what it looked and felt like. This is you looking at and feeling the part of you that is now leaving to allow space for the new parts now growing in you. You are beginning transformation and it is just this simple.

When you become accustomed to this process it will be easier and easier for you to view your old parts as they leave. It will become easier and easier for you to be who you are without the interference of old beliefs who once owned you. You will be free of your outdated and limited self and you will expand in all directions and all areas of your life. You are now moving at a pace that is rather rapid and may sometimes startle you. You will learn to deal with this new pace, or vibration, and you will learn to know how you are not only 'not' out of control, you are actually being very strongly guided.

You are beginning to move into a space that will allow you to be more of you and to rise above this lowly opinion you have of yourself. You are taking on many changes at this time and you do not realize that this is exactly how you transform and move up to higher levels of consciousness. As you move up to higher levels I wish you to stay calm and not get too excited. Sometimes you give your good away by becoming over exuberant in your reaction to your new found awareness. This can cause you to begin to doubt what you have just become aware of.

You are moving quickly now and you are making wonderful progress. You, of course, are not inside of you and so you cannot see this progress but it is there. You will begin to see it soon and it will begin to reflect onto your outer world. You are very much like a shadow that is moving, as the sun hits the object that is casting the shadow from all directions. You will soon come full circle and begin to see how your shadow shortens as the sun rises higher and higher in the sky. This is how you are rising up. Your shadow is becoming smaller and smaller, until you will no longer see your shadow due to the fact that the light is shining directly above you. This will be your own light and it will lead you on to peace. No more shadows to walk through. Only peace.

⁂

You are not only beginning to change, you are beginning to feel like you are no longer "settled." You are beginning to feel unrest within you and this will lead you to your goal. Your goal is to walk to the light. Your goal is to become what you once were. Your goal is to become "all that is" and your goal is to know that you are God. You are tired of living a lie and you wish to know the truth. The truth is simply "all that is" and you wish to know "all that is."

You are coming out of a very long and very deep sleep, and as you do so you will learn to rise above the dream and even the nightmares. You are coming to and you are rising above what you once believed in order to have a new belief. Do not get stuck in your new belief. Let it go when you are ready to move to your next level or next belief system. This does not mean you are crazy or fickle. This simply means you are moving and changing. Allow this to be okay. In the same way that a cliff climber will let go of one hold to grab on to a new hold, you will let go of one belief and grab on to a new belief or new way of seeing your world. In the end you will no longer require a belief system nor will you require anything to believe in.

For now, however, we must allow you to be where you are and that allows you to hold on to your beliefs and not push them at others. This will assist you when the time to change your mind occurs, and you will be able to move on more easily. You see, when you push your beliefs at others you get even more stuck in them. Whatever you fight for or defend becomes yours in certain ways. As we begin to show you what you have been fighting for and sticking to, you will begin to see how you no longer wish to be stuck to, or in, these areas. It is best to let go of your desire to have strong opinions, as you are in actuality *all* opinions. You are "all that is" and to accept only one view limits you to one portion of you. Your ideal goal is to become and accept all of you, which makes having a set opinion or point of view very unnecessary.

So, as we move on into our next grade, I wish you to remember that you are all things and not limited. You *are* all points of view and you *are* all possibilities. So if you put down a possibility, or a point of view, you are putting down that part of you. Do not cut "you" off in this fashion. Begin to know you and begin to love and accept all parts of you.

You are now moving on to our next level of awareness. I will end this book now as I know you will be ready to put into practice the insights taught here. You are moving quite rapidly now, and your awareness and your ability to accept is expanding. Our next book will be titled *Illumination*. This is Liane's choice for a title and I agree that it is a good one. We will see you back here next semester for more enlightening, lifting and illuminating information. Until then, be good to yourself for you are all you have.

God's Pen

I first heard the voice of God in 1988. I was sitting in my back yard reading a book when this big booming voice interrupted with, "I am God and I will not come to you by any other name." I felt like the voice was everywhere – inside of me as well as in the sky around me. I was so frightened that I ran in my bedroom to hide.

This was not the first time that I heard voices. I had been communicating with my own spirit guide or soul for about a year. I guess my depth of fear regarding God, and all that he represented to me at the time, was just too much.

I spent two days trying to avoid the voice of God, which was patiently waiting for me to respond. By the second day I was exhausted from lack of sleep and decided to give in and talk with him. This turned out to be the greatest gift and best decision of my life.

The first book, *God Spoke through Me to Tell You to Speak to Him*, shows my evolution from communicating with my soul to communicating with the Big Guy. It took a couple years for me to be comfortable communicating with God. My fear of a punishing God was big! That has most definitely changed and I now think of God as my partner and best friend.

In the beginning the voice of God would wake me in the middle of the night and tell me it was time to write. He said I had promised to do this work (I assumed he was talking about the soul/spirit me). I would drag myself up to a sitting position and watch in amazement as my hand flew across the page, while I tried to keep up by reading what was being written.

It was always so much fun to wake up the next morning and grab my notebook to see what God had written during the night. After some time the voice stopped waking me and I became comfortable picking up my pen and writing for God first thing in the morning. I think in the beginning I had to be awakened while still semi-conscious from sleep so I wouldn't object too much to the information that was being channeled through me.

As I grew less and less afraid (and more trusting) of God, he was able to communicate greater information. Some of the information is quit controversial, but I felt it important to just let it be and not censor it. I present the writings here to you as they were given to me. I have edited a little (mostly the more personal information regarding myself) and I have used a pen name for privacy reasons. I asked God for a good pen name and he guided me to Liane which (I was told) in Hebrew means "God has answered."

At one point I became a little concerned about my sanity in all this, so I went to a hypnotherapist to find out what I was doing. Under hypnosis I saw this incredibly huge beam of light with a voice coming from within it. It was a giant "loving light" and felt so comforting and kind. It felt like that's where I came from. After that I stopped worrying about my sanity. If this is crazy, I think it's a very good kind of crazy to be....

In loving light, Liane

Loving Light Books

Available at:
Loving Light Books: www.lovinglightbooks.com
Amazon: www.amazon.com
Barnes & Noble: www.barnesandnoble.com

Also Available on Request at Local Bookstores

www.ingramcontent.com/pod-product-compliance
Lightning Source LLC
Chambersburg PA
CBHW031844090426
42741CB00005B/340